THE ANGEL OF MARYE'S HEIGHTS

A GRAPHIC NOVEL BIOGRAPHY OF
RICHARD ROWLAND KIRKLAND

WRITTEN BY NEL YOMTOV   ILLUSTRATED BY DANTE GINEVRA

CAPSTONE PRESS

Published by Capstone Press, an imprint of Capstone
1710 Roe Crest Drive, North Mankato, Minnesota 56003
capstonepub.com

Library of Congress Cataloging-in-Publication Data is available on the Library of
Congress website.

ISBN: 9781669061755 (hardcover)
ISBN: 9781669061885 (paperback)
ISBN: 9781669061793 (ebook PDF)

Summary: At age 19, Confederate soldier Richard Rowland Kirkland fought in the
brutal Battle of Fredericksburg during the U.S. Civil War. Witnessing the suffering
of Union soldiers, Kirkland was moved to show compassion. Putting his own life at
risk, Kirkland took water to the weakened men on the battlefield.

Editorial Credits
Editor: Julie Gassman; Designer: Dina Her; Production Specialist: Tori Abraham

Image Credit
Wikimedia: Public Domain, 28

Printed and bound in the USA. 5626

TABLE OF CONTENTS

Desperate for Victory

The American Civil War (1861–1865)

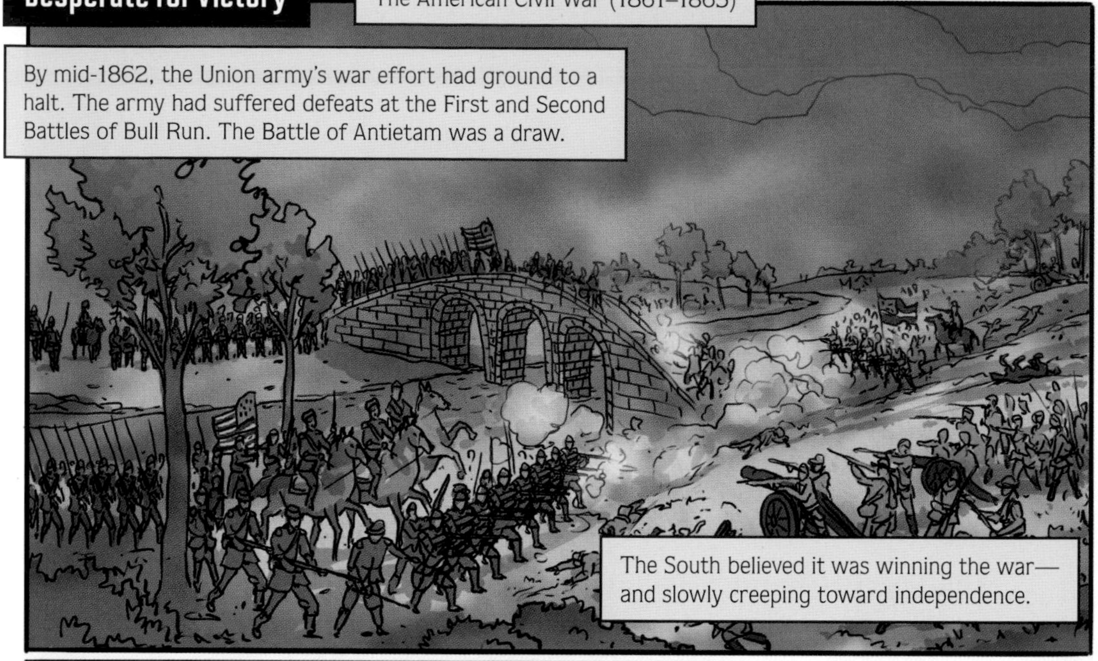
By mid-1862, the Union army's war effort had ground to a halt. The army had suffered defeats at the First and Second Battles of Bull Run. The Battle of Antietam was a draw.
The South believed it was winning the war—and slowly creeping toward independence.

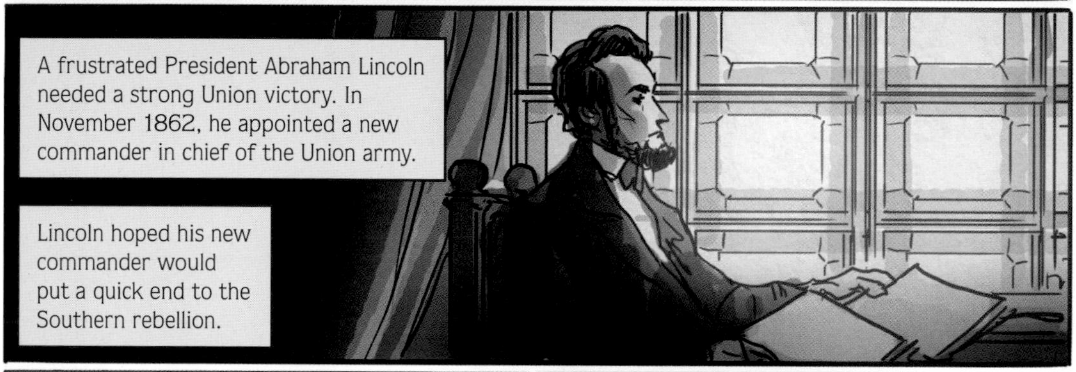
A frustrated President Abraham Lincoln needed a strong Union victory. In November 1862, he appointed a new commander in chief of the Union army.
Lincoln hoped his new commander would put a quick end to the Southern rebellion.

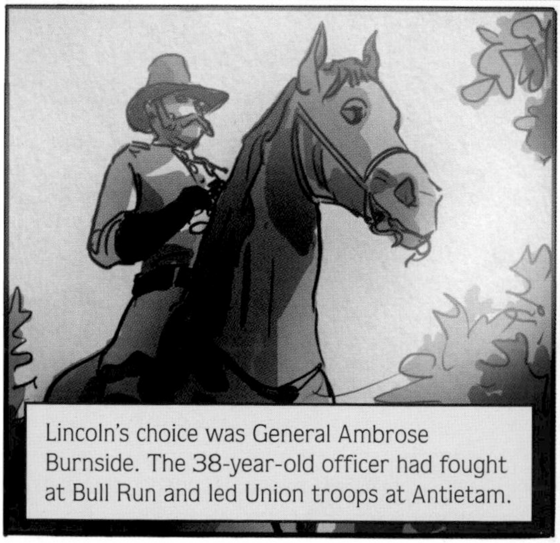
Lincoln's choice was General Ambrose Burnside. The 38-year-old officer had fought at Bull Run and led Union troops at Antietam.

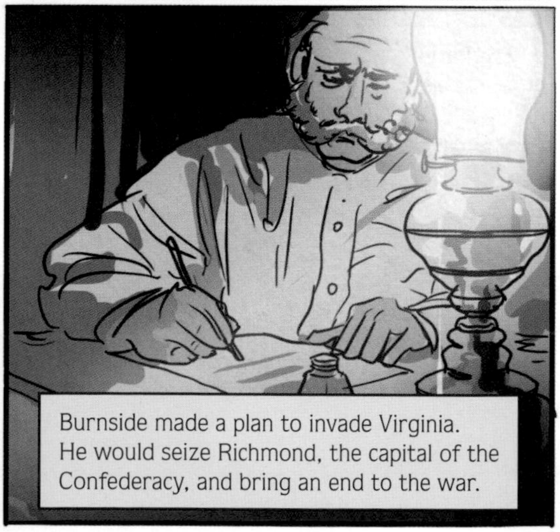
Burnside made a plan to invade Virginia. He would seize Richmond, the capital of the Confederacy, and bring an end to the war.

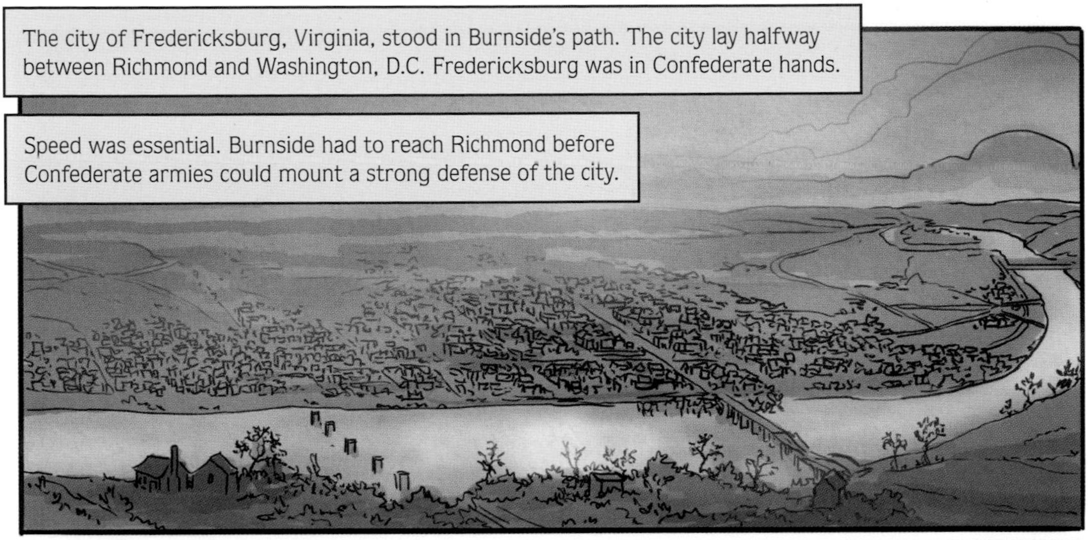
The city of Fredericksburg, Virginia, stood in Burnside's path. The city lay halfway between Richmond and Washington, D.C. Fredericksburg was in Confederate hands.
Speed was essential. Burnside had to reach Richmond before Confederate armies could mount a strong defense of the city.

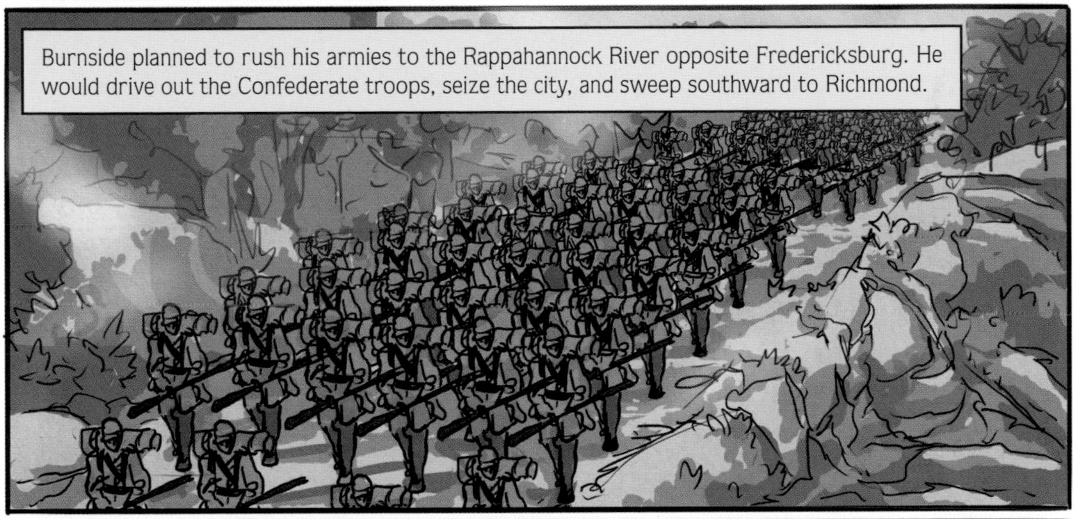
Burnside planned to rush his armies to the Rappahannock River opposite Fredericksburg. He would drive out the Confederate troops, seize the city, and sweep southward to Richmond.

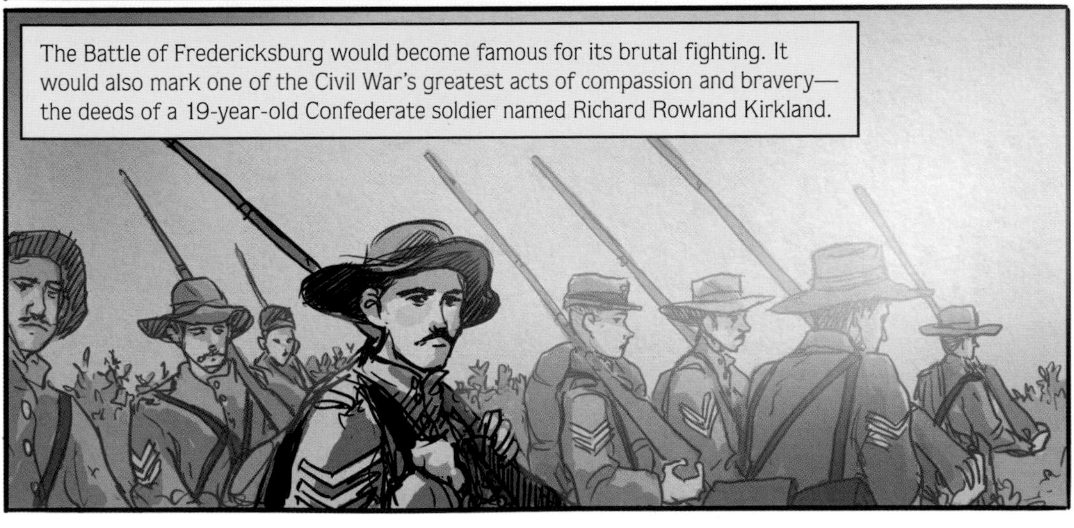
The Battle of Fredericksburg would become famous for its brutal fighting. It would also mark one of the Civil War's greatest acts of compassion and bravery—the deeds of a 19-year-old Confederate soldier named Richard Rowland Kirkland.

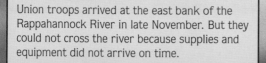

Union troops arrived at the east bank of the Rappahannock River in late November. But they could not cross the river because supplies and equipment did not arrive on time.

Many days passed. Finally, on December 11, Union troops began crossing the river.

The delay gave Confederate general Robert E. Lee time to strengthen his position around Fredericksburg.

By December 11, the Confederate line of 78,000 troops stretched about 20 miles (32 kilometers). It ran from Prospect Hill in the south to Marye's* Heights overlooking Fredericksburg in the north.

*Pronounced "Marie's"

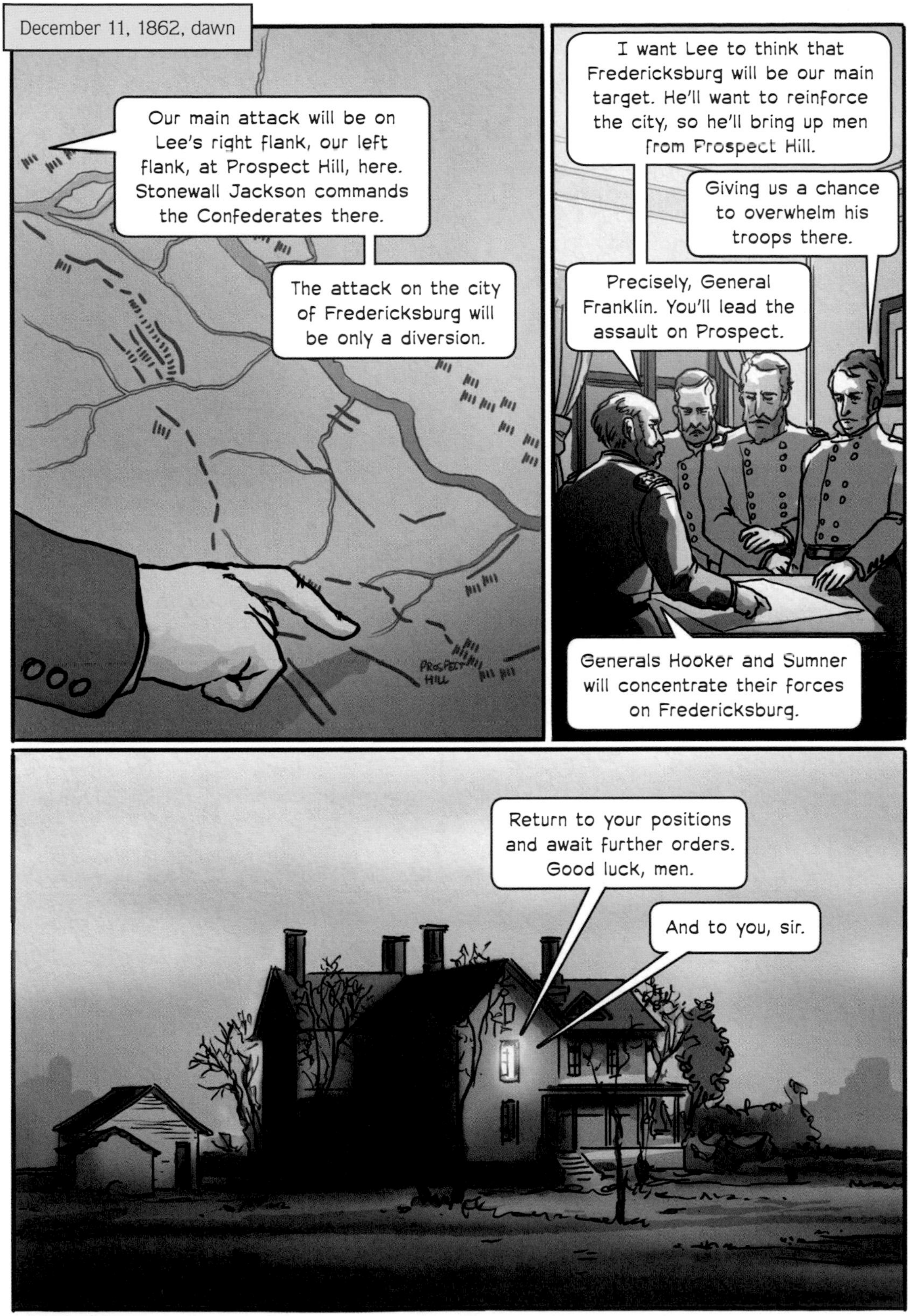
December 11, 1862, dawn
Our main attack will be on Lee's right flank, our left flank, at Prospect Hill, here. Stonewall Jackson commands the Confederates there.
The attack on the city of Fredericksburg will be only a diversion.
PROSPECT HILL
I want Lee to think that Fredericksburg will be our main target. He'll want to reinforce the city, so he'll bring up men from Prospect Hill.
Giving us a chance to overwhelm his troops there.
Precisely, General Franklin. You'll lead the assault on Prospect.
Generals Hooker and Sumner will concentrate their forces on Fredericksburg.
Return to your positions and await further orders. Good luck, men.
And to you, sir.

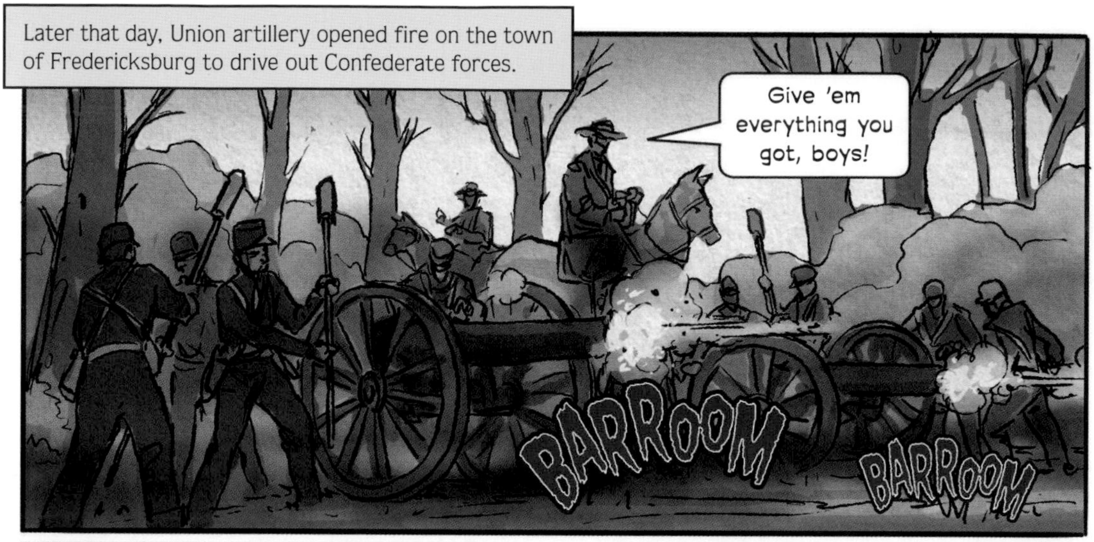
Later that day, Union artillery opened fire on the town of Fredericksburg to drive out Confederate forces.
Give 'em everything you got, boys!
BARROOM
BARROOM

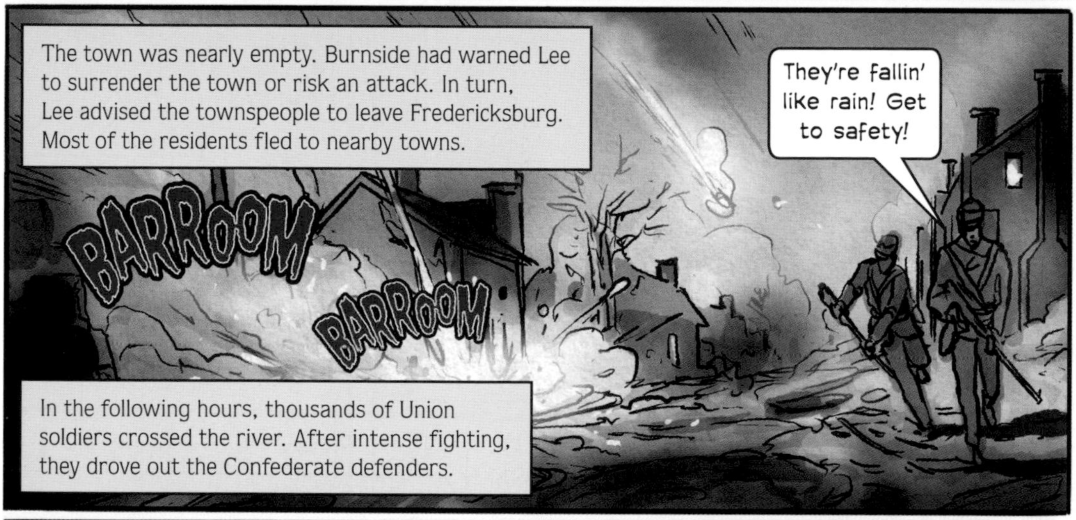
The town was nearly empty. Burnside had warned Lee to surrender the town or risk an attack. In turn, Lee advised the townspeople to leave Fredericksburg. Most of the residents fled to nearby towns.
They're fallin' like rain! Get to safety!
BARROOM
BARROOM
In the following hours, thousands of Union soldiers crossed the river. After intense fighting, they drove out the Confederate defenders.

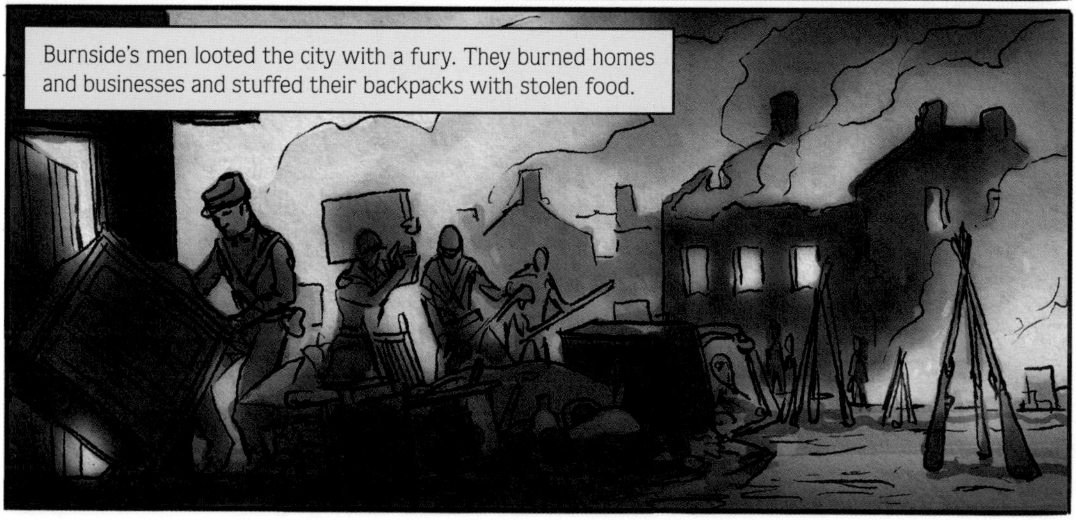
Burnside's men looted the city with a fury. They burned homes and businesses and stuffed their backpacks with stolen food.

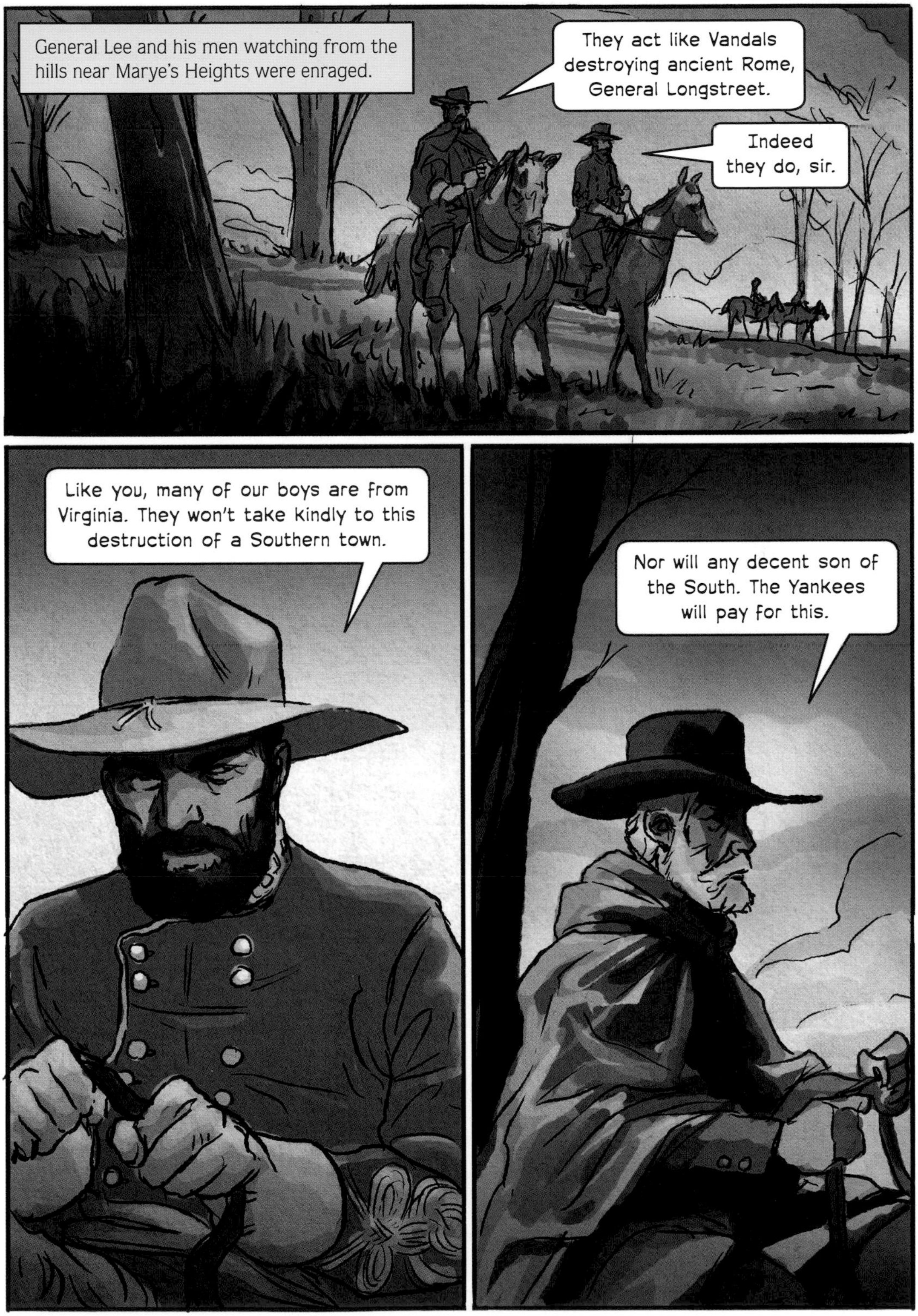
General Lee and his men watching from the hills near Marye's Heights were enraged.
They act like Vandals destroying ancient Rome, General Longstreet.
Indeed they do, sir.
Like you, many of our boys are from Virginia. They won't take kindly to this destruction of a Southern town.
Nor will any decent son of the South. The Yankees will pay for this.

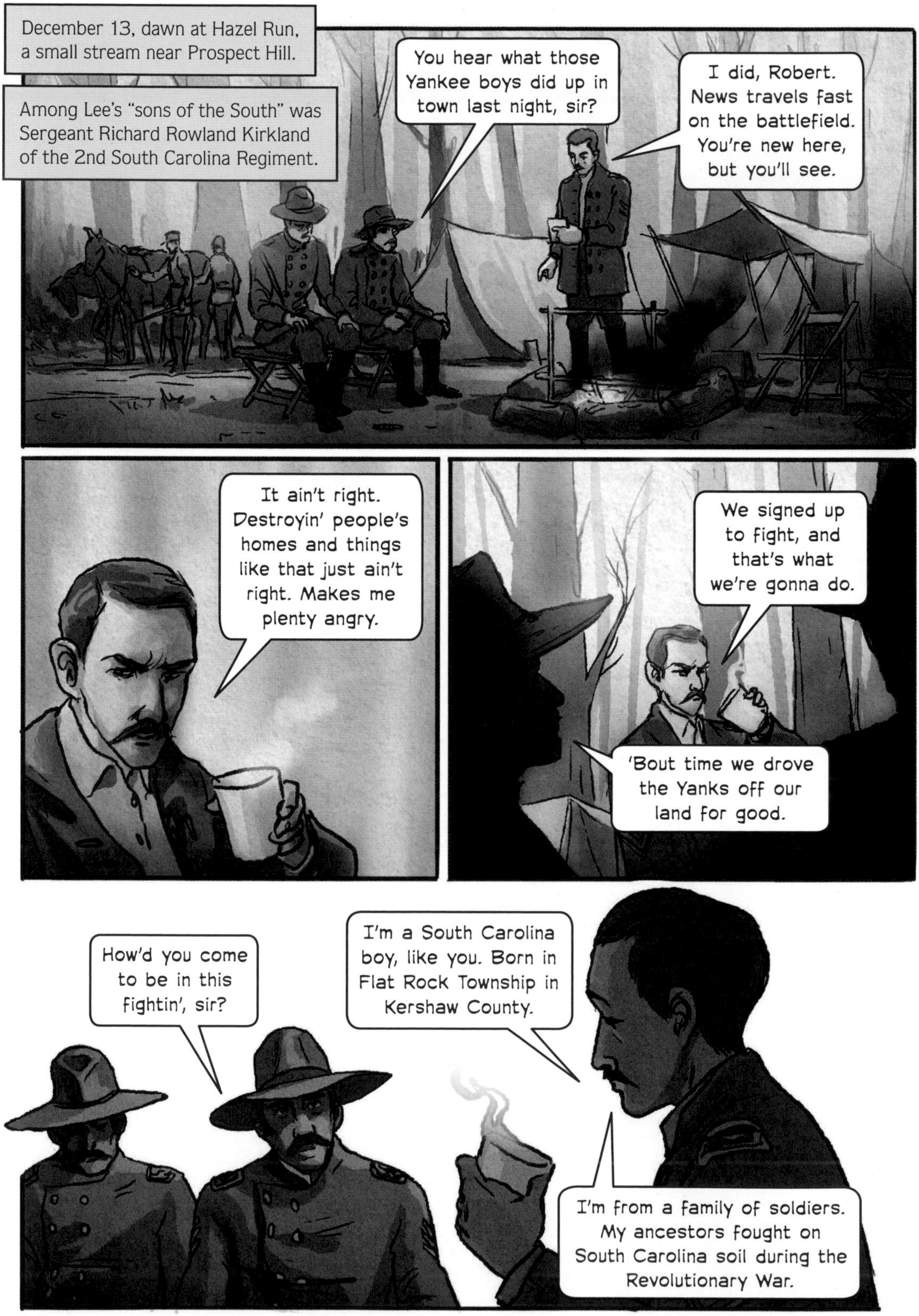

December 13, dawn at Hazel Run, a small stream near Prospect Hill.
Among Lee's "sons of the South" was Sergeant Richard Rowland Kirkland of the 2nd South Carolina Regiment.
You hear what those Yankee boys did up in town last night, sir?
I did, Robert. News travels fast on the battlefield. You're new here, but you'll see.
It ain't right. Destroyin' people's homes and things like that just ain't right. Makes me plenty angry.
We signed up to fight, and that's what we're gonna do.
'Bout time we drove the Yanks off our land for good.
How'd you come to be in this fightin', sir?
I'm a South Carolina boy, like you. Born in Flat Rock Township in Kershaw County.
I'm from a family of soldiers. My ancestors fought on South Carolina soil during the Revolutionary War.

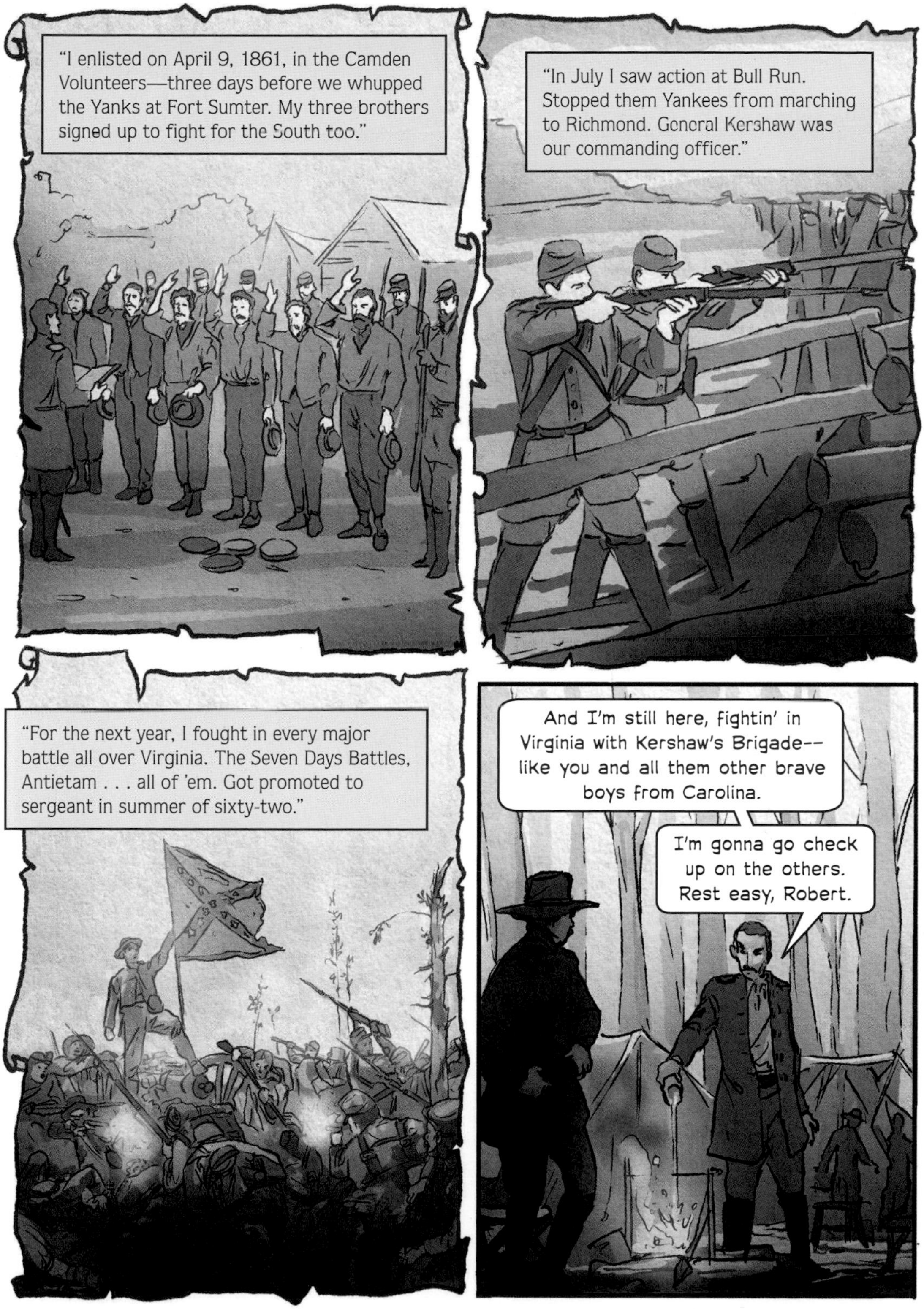
"I enlisted on April 9, 1861, in the Camden Volunteers—three days before we whupped the Yanks at Fort Sumter. My three brothers signed up to fight for the South too."
"In July I saw action at Bull Run. Stopped them Yankees from marching to Richmond. General Kershaw was our commanding officer."
"For the next year, I fought in every major battle all over Virginia. The Seven Days Battles, Antietam . . . all of 'em. Got promoted to sergeant in summer of sixty-two."
And I'm still here, fightin' in Virginia with Kershaw's Brigade--like you and all them other brave boys from Carolina.
I'm gonna go check up on the others. Rest easy, Robert.

Into the Jaws of Death

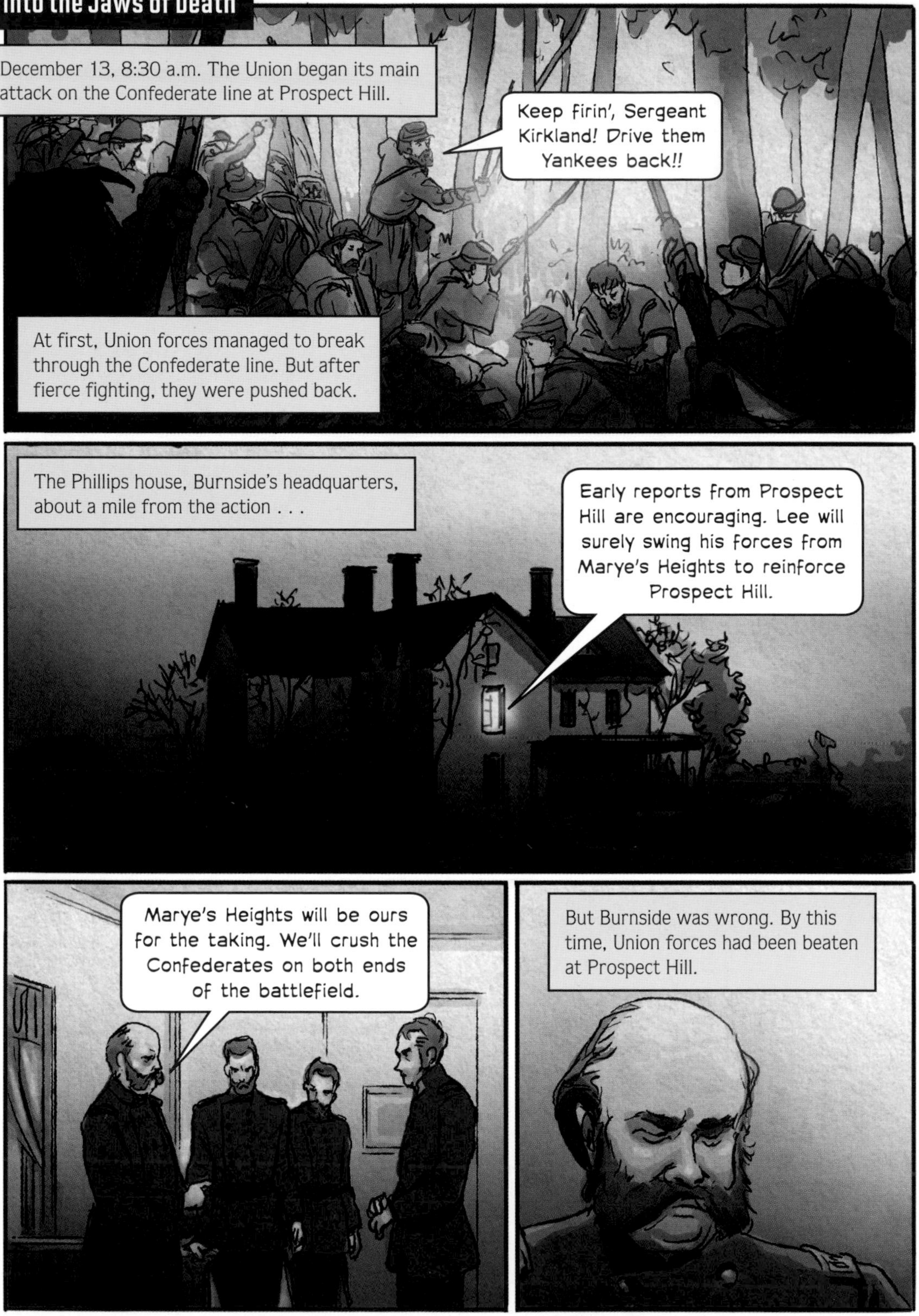

December 13, 8:30 a.m. The Union began its main attack on the Confederate line at Prospect Hill.
Keep firin', Sergeant Kirkland! Drive them Yankees back!!
At first, Union forces managed to break through the Confederate line. But after fierce fighting, they were pushed back.
The Phillips house, Burnside's headquarters, about a mile from the action . . .
Early reports from Prospect Hill are encouraging. Lee will surely swing his forces from Marye's Heights to reinforce Prospect Hill.
Marye's Heights will be ours for the taking. We'll crush the Confederates on both ends of the battlefield.
But Burnside was wrong. By this time, Union forces had been beaten at Prospect Hill.

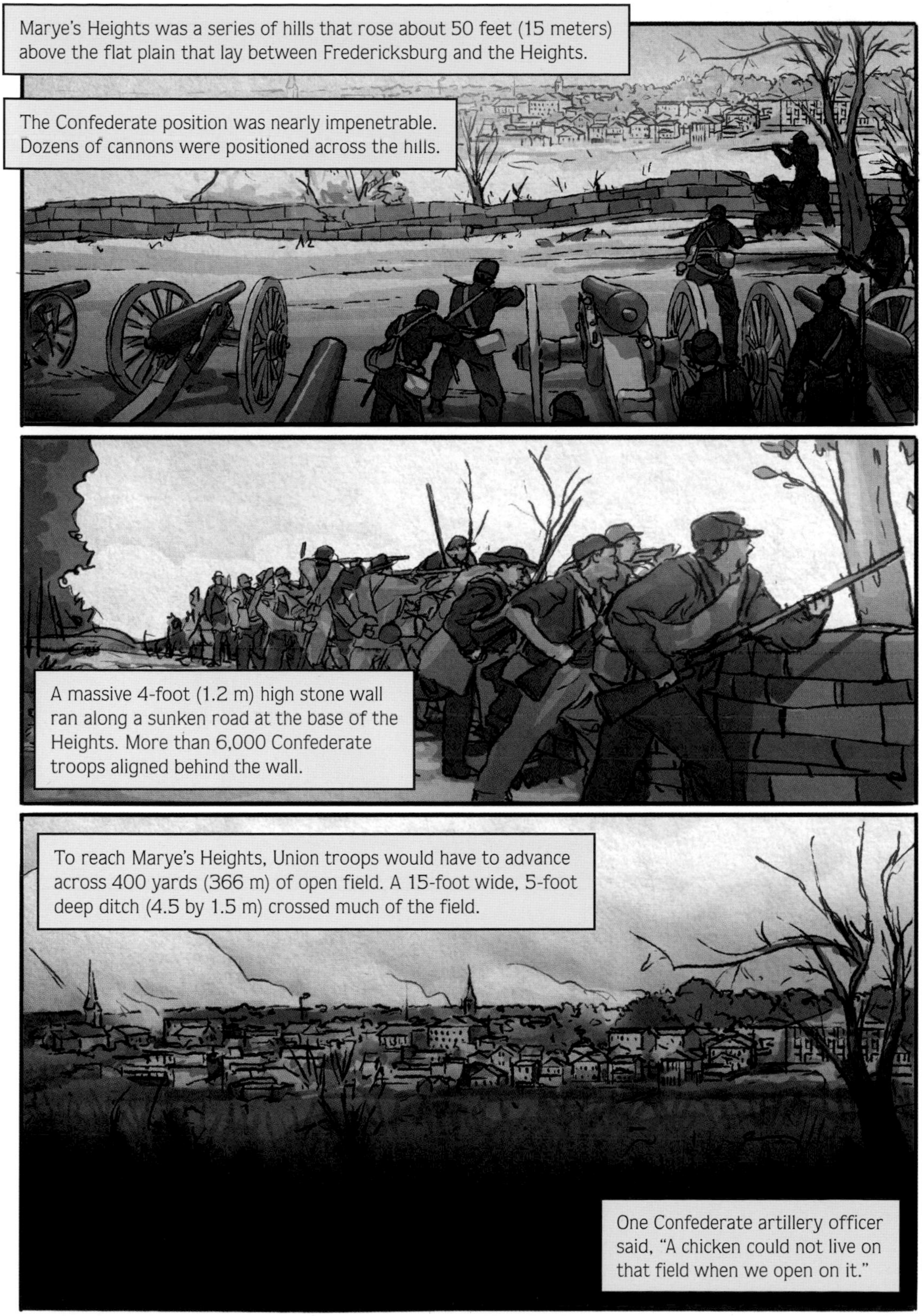
Marye's Heights was a series of hills that rose about 50 feet (15 meters) above the flat plain that lay between Fredericksburg and the Heights.
The Confederate position was nearly impenetrable. Dozens of cannons were positioned across the hills.
A massive 4-foot (1.2 m) high stone wall ran along a sunken road at the base of the Heights. More than 6,000 Confederate troops aligned behind the wall.
To reach Marye's Heights, Union troops would have to advance across 400 yards (366 m) of open field. A 15-foot wide, 5-foot deep ditch (4.5 by 1.5 m) crossed much of the field.
One Confederate artillery officer said, "A chicken could not live on that field when we open on it."

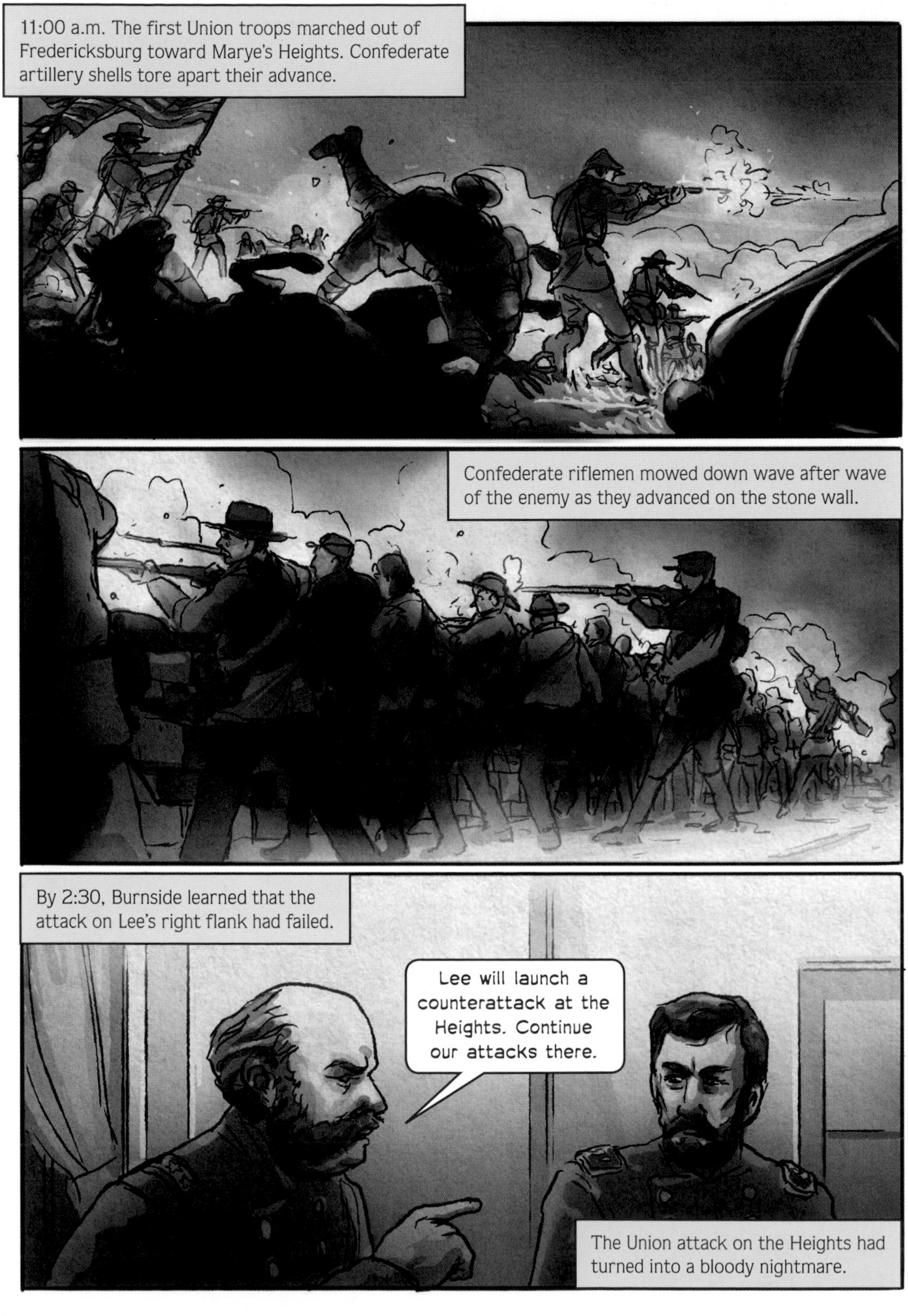
11:00 a.m. The first Union troops marched out of Fredericksburg toward Marye's Heights. Confederate artillery shells tore apart their advance.
Confederate riflemen mowed down wave after wave of the enemy as they advanced on the stone wall.
By 2:30, Burnside learned that the attack on Lee's right flank had failed.
Lee will launch a counterattack at the Heights. Continue our attacks there.
The Union attack on the Heights had turned into a bloody nightmare.

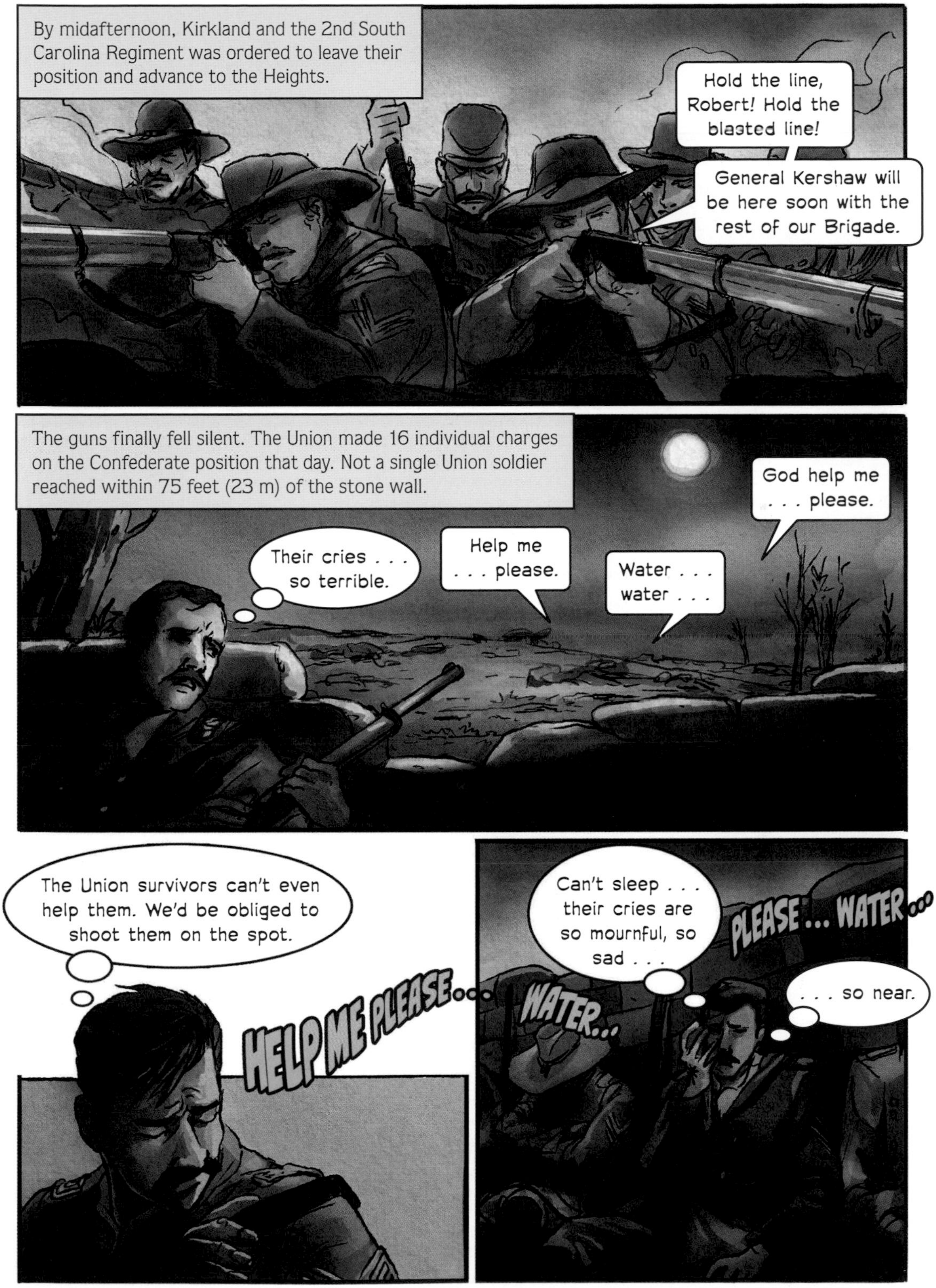
By midafternoon, Kirkland and the 2nd South Carolina Regiment was ordered to leave their position and advance to the Heights.
Hold the line, Robert! Hold the blasted line!
General Kershaw will be here soon with the rest of our Brigade.
The guns finally fell silent. The Union made 16 individual charges on the Confederate position that day. Not a single Union soldier reached within 75 feet (23 m) of the stone wall.
Their cries . . . so terrible.
Help me . . . please.
Water . . . water . . .
God help me . . . please.
The Union survivors can't even help them. We'd be obliged to shoot them on the spot.
HELP ME PLEASE...
Can't sleep . . . their cries are so mournful, so sad . . .
WATER...
PLEASE... WATER...
. . . so near.

Mission of Mercy

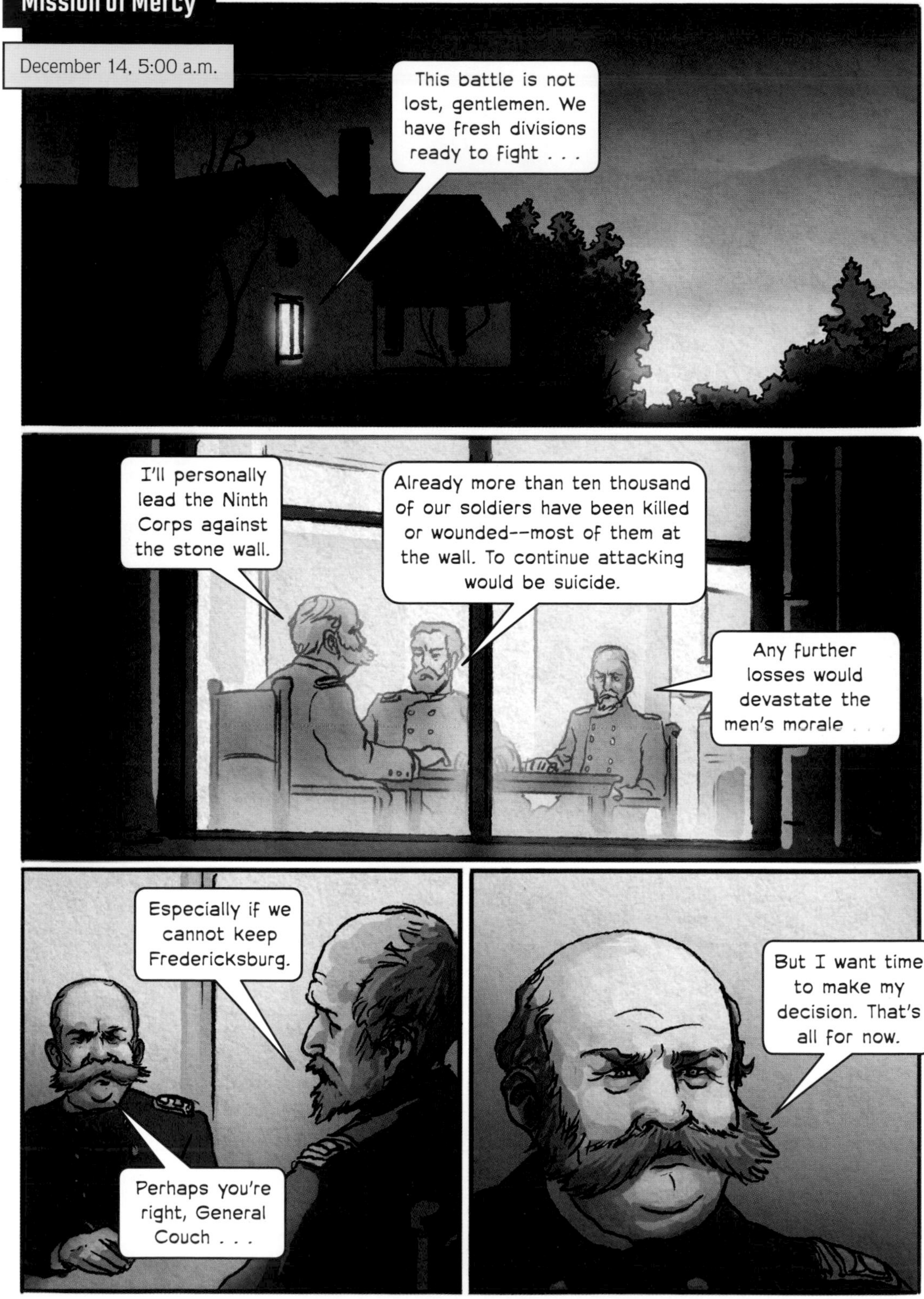
December 14, 5:00 a.m.
This battle is not lost, gentlemen. We have fresh divisions ready to fight . . .
I'll personally lead the Ninth Corps against the stone wall.
Already more than ten thousand of our soldiers have been killed or wounded--most of them at the wall. To continue attacking would be suicide.
Any further losses would devastate the men's morale . . .
Especially if we cannot keep Fredericksburg.
Perhaps you're right, General Couch . . .
But I want time to make my decision. That's all for now.

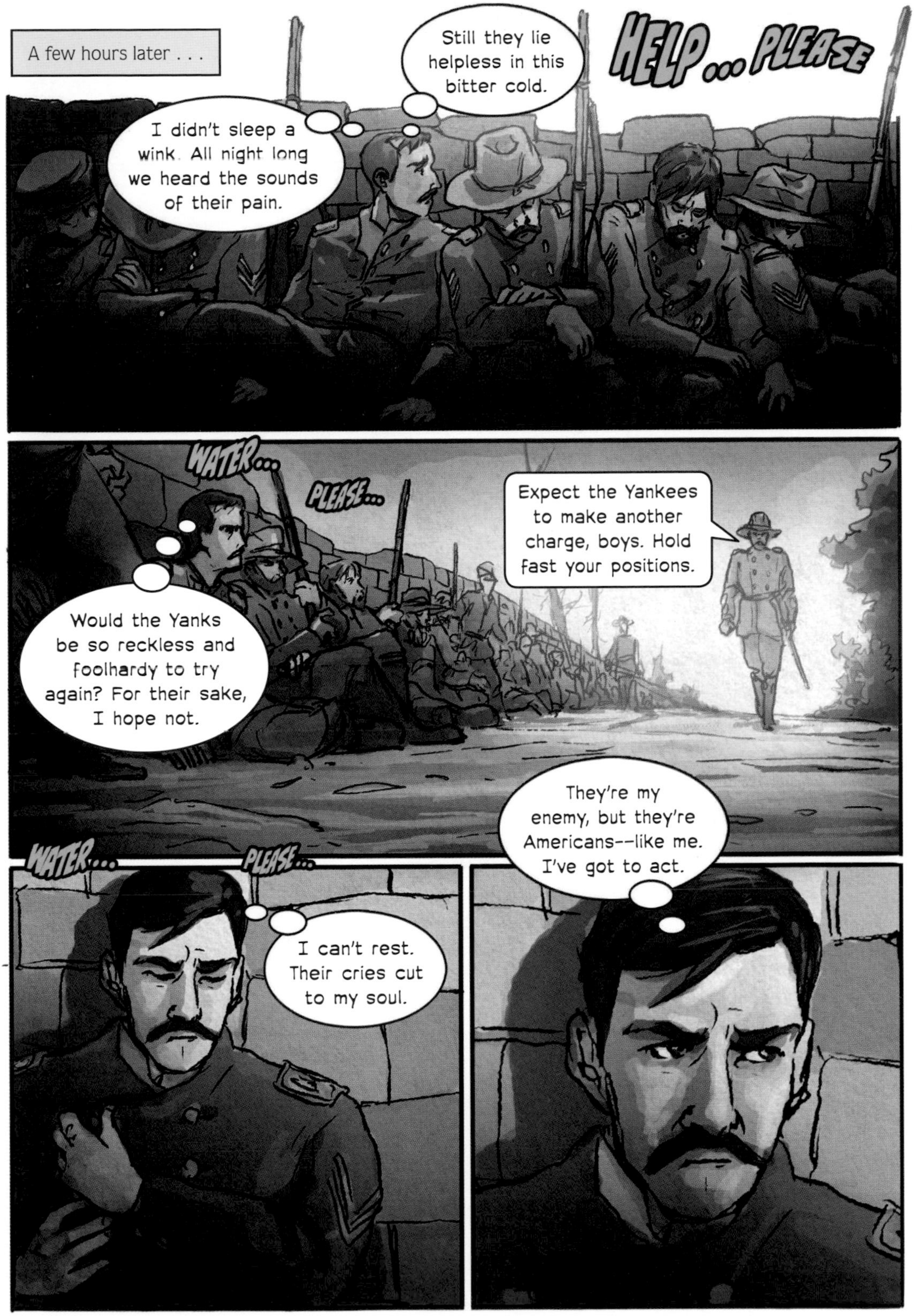
A few hours later . . .
Still they lie helpless in this bitter cold.
HELP . . . PLEASE
I didn't sleep a wink. All night long we heard the sounds of their pain.
WATER . . .
PLEASE . . .
Expect the Yankees to make another charge, boys. Hold fast your positions.
Would the Yanks be so reckless and foolhardy to try again? For their sake, I hope not.
WATER . . .
PLEASE . . .
I can't rest. Their cries cut to my soul.
They're my enemy, but they're Americans--like me. I've got to act.

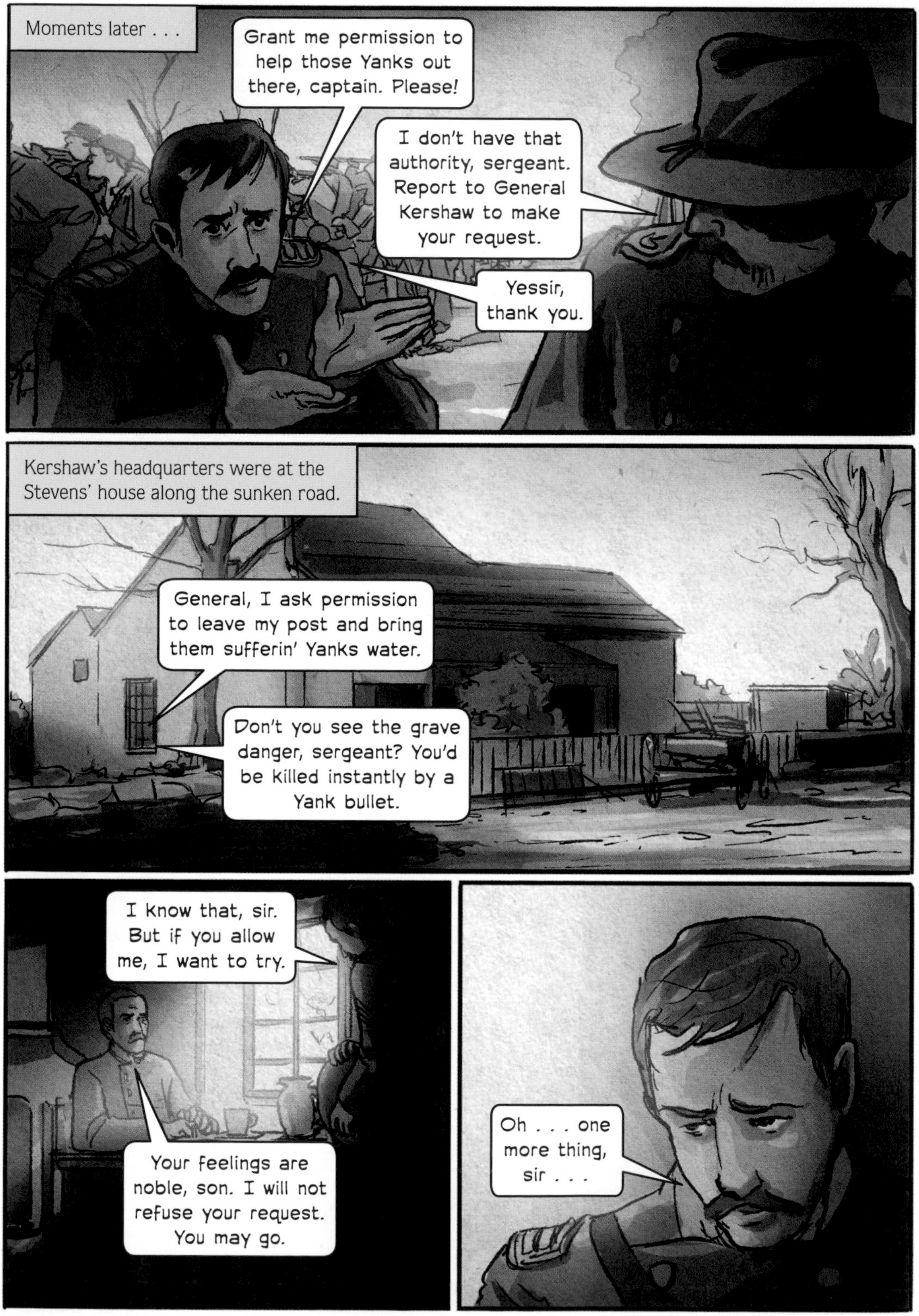
Moments later . . .
Grant me permission to help those Yanks out there, captain. Please!
I don't have that authority, sergeant. Report to General Kershaw to make your request.
Yessir, thank you.
Kershaw's headquarters were at the Stevens' house along the sunken road.
General, I ask permission to leave my post and bring them sufferin' Yanks water.
Don't you see the grave danger, sergeant? You'd be killed instantly by a Yank bullet.
I know that, sir. But if you allow me, I want to try.
Your feelings are noble, son. I will not refuse your request. You may go.
Oh . . . one more thing, sir . . .

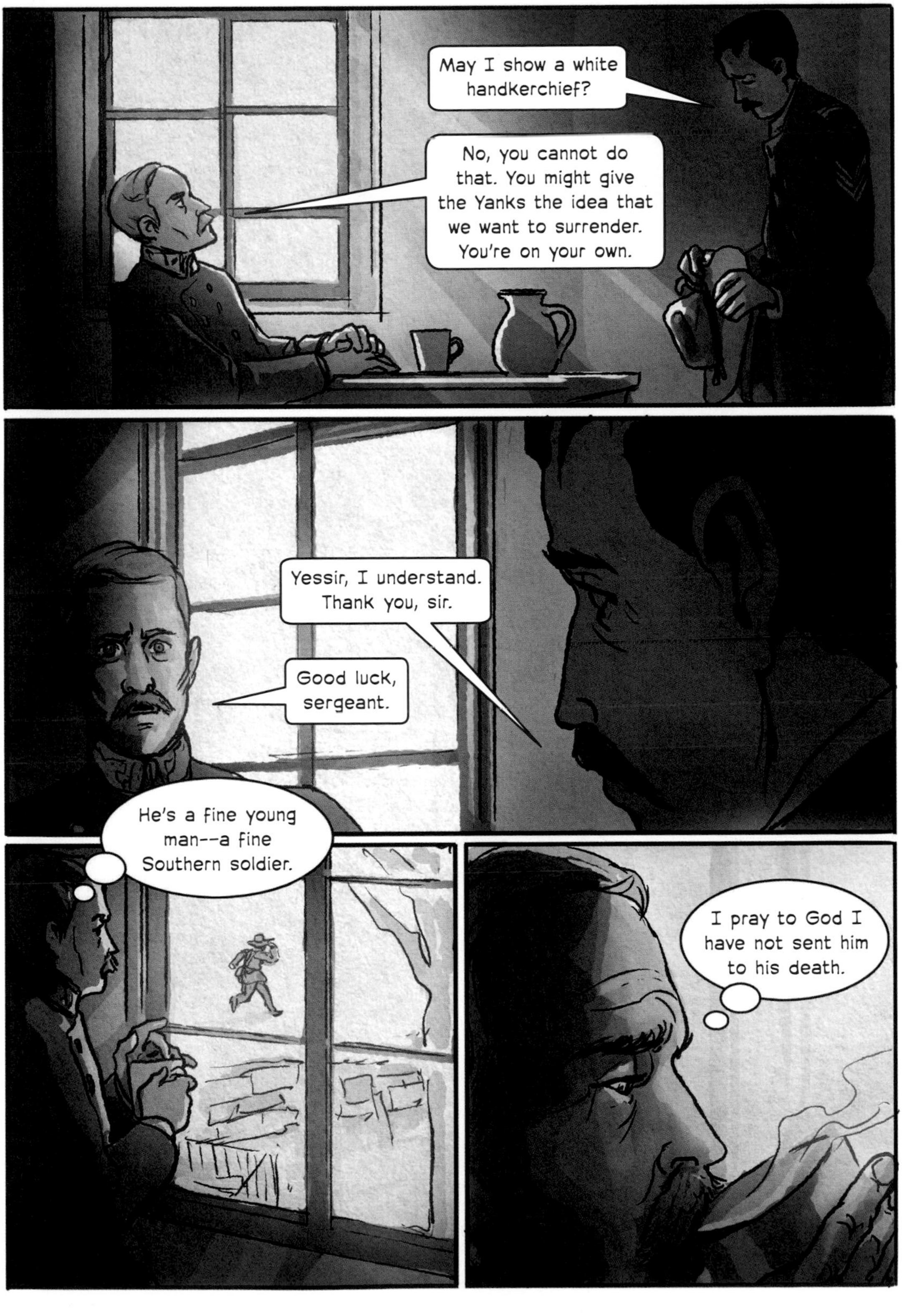
May I show a white handkerchief?
No, you cannot do that. You might give the Yanks the idea that we want to surrender. You're on your own.
Yessir, I understand. Thank you, sir.
Good luck, sergeant.
He's a fine young man--a fine Southern soldier.
I pray to God I have not sent him to his death.

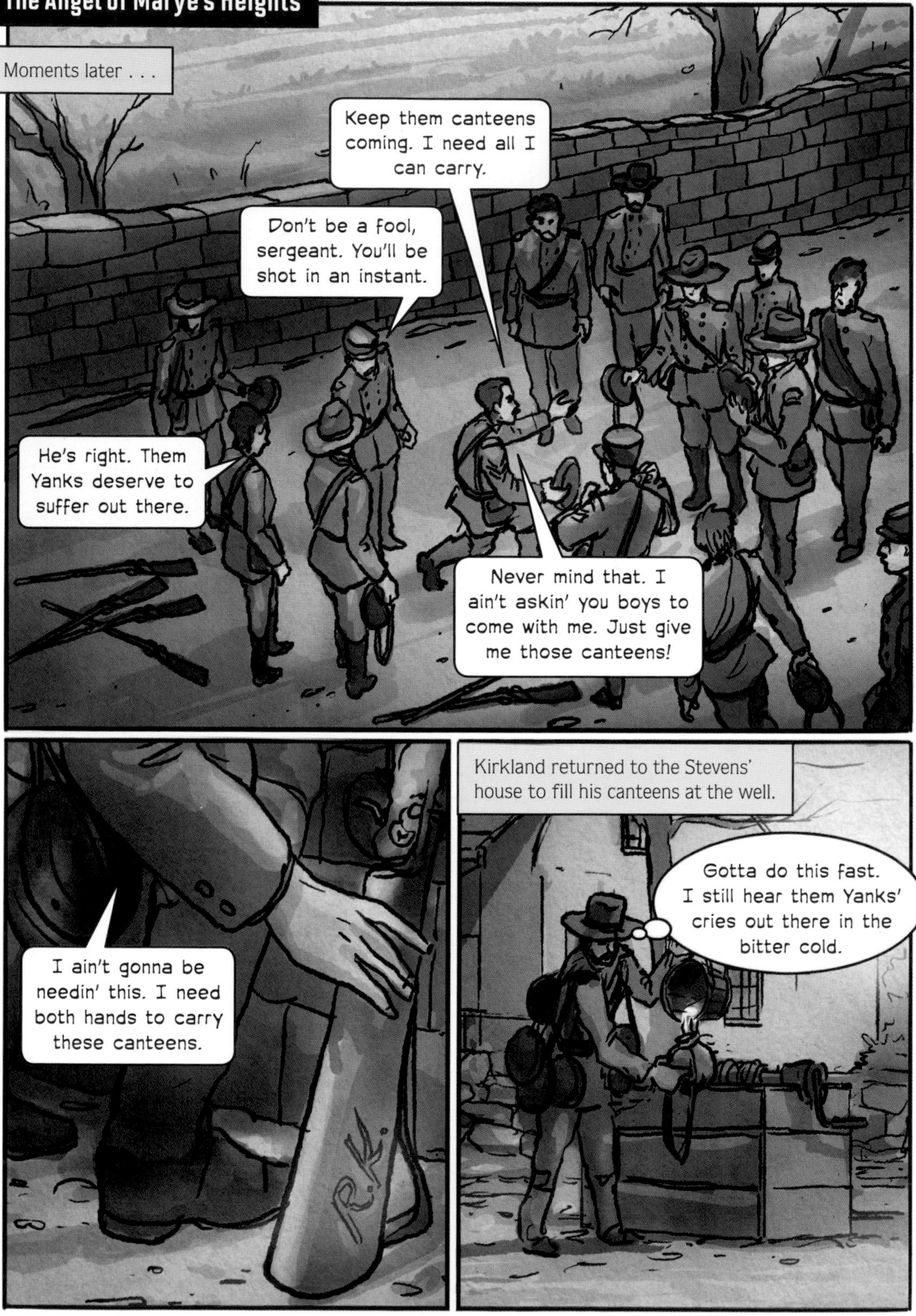
Moments later . . .
Keep them canteens coming. I need all I can carry.
Don't be a fool, sergeant. You'll be shot in an instant.
He's right. Them Yanks deserve to suffer out there.
Never mind that. I ain't askin' you boys to come with me. Just give me those canteens!
I ain't gonna be needin' this. I need both hands to carry these canteens.
Kirkland returned to the Stevens' house to fill his canteens at the well.
Gotta do this fast. I still hear them Yanks' cries out there in the bitter cold.

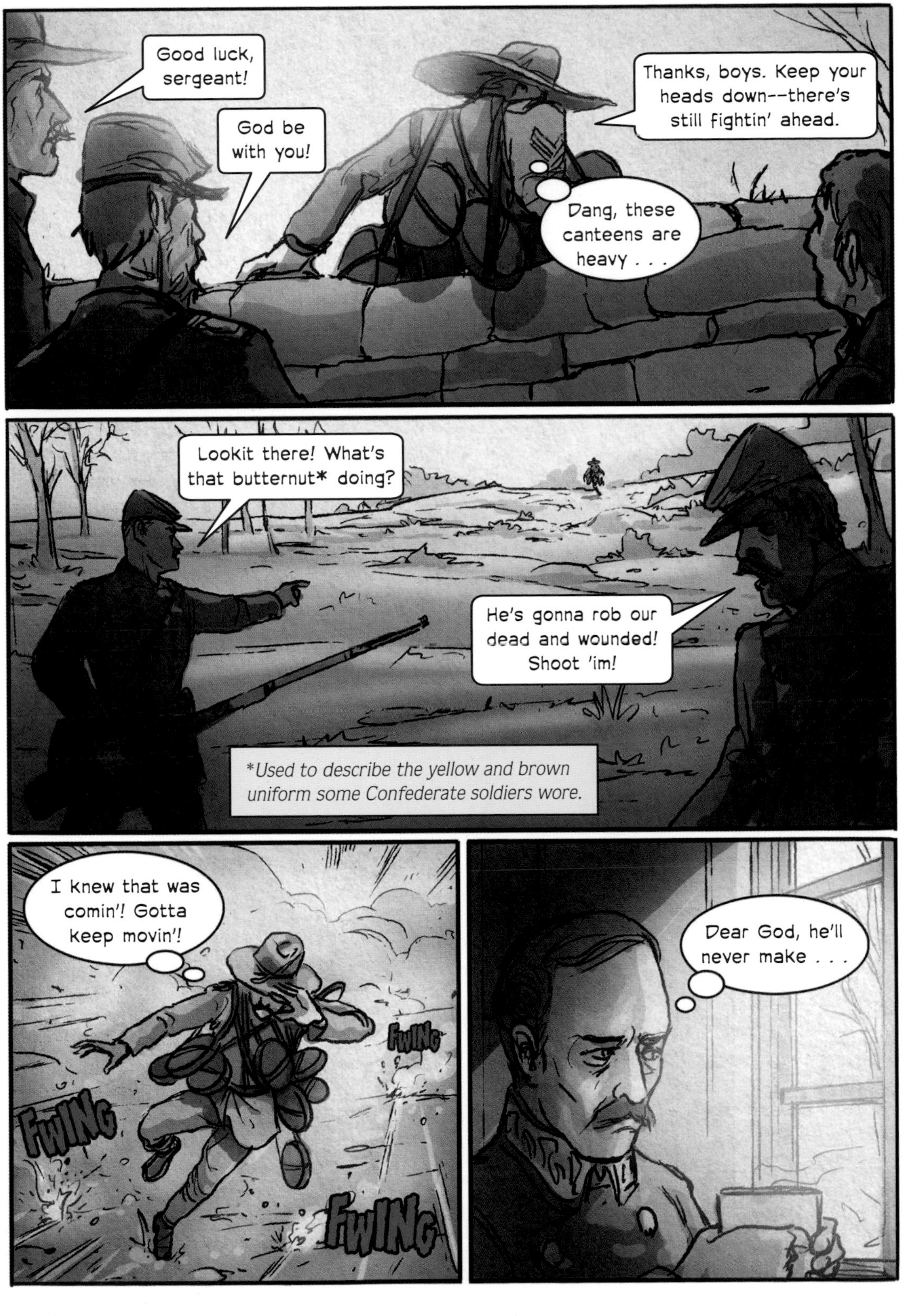
Good luck, sergeant!
God be with you!
Thanks, boys. Keep your heads down--there's still fightin' ahead.
Dang, these canteens are heavy . . .
Lookit there! What's that butternut* doing?
He's gonna rob our dead and wounded! Shoot 'im!
*Used to describe the yellow and brown uniform some Confederate soldiers wore.
I knew that was comin'! Gotta keep movin'!
FWING
FWING
FWING
Dear God, he'll never make . . .

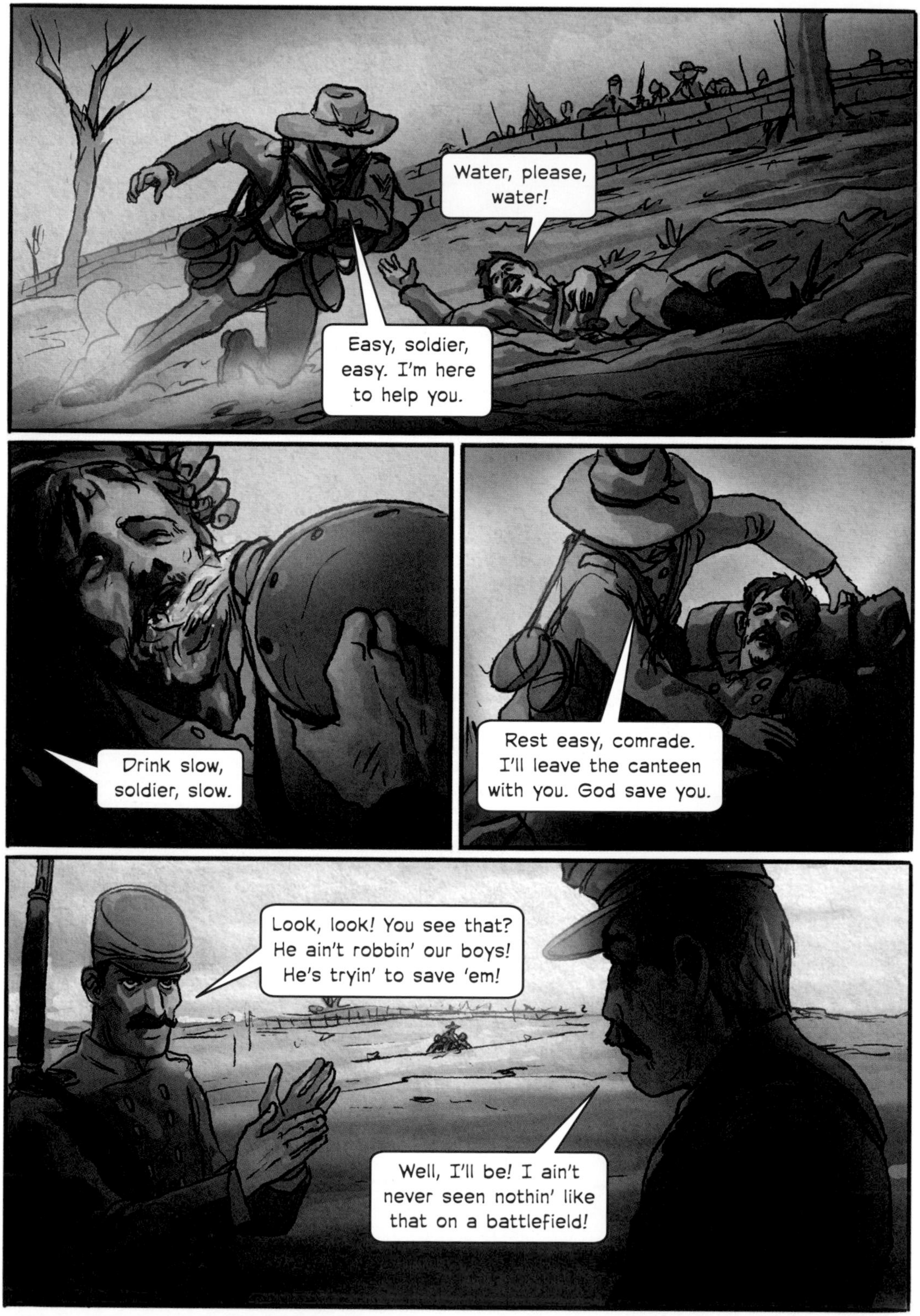
Water, please, water!
Easy, soldier, easy. I'm here to help you.
Drink slow, soldier, slow.
Rest easy, comrade. I'll leave the canteen with you. God save you.
Look, look! You see that? He ain't robbin' our boys! He's tryin' to save 'em!
Well, I'll be! I ain't never seen nothin' like that on a battlefield!

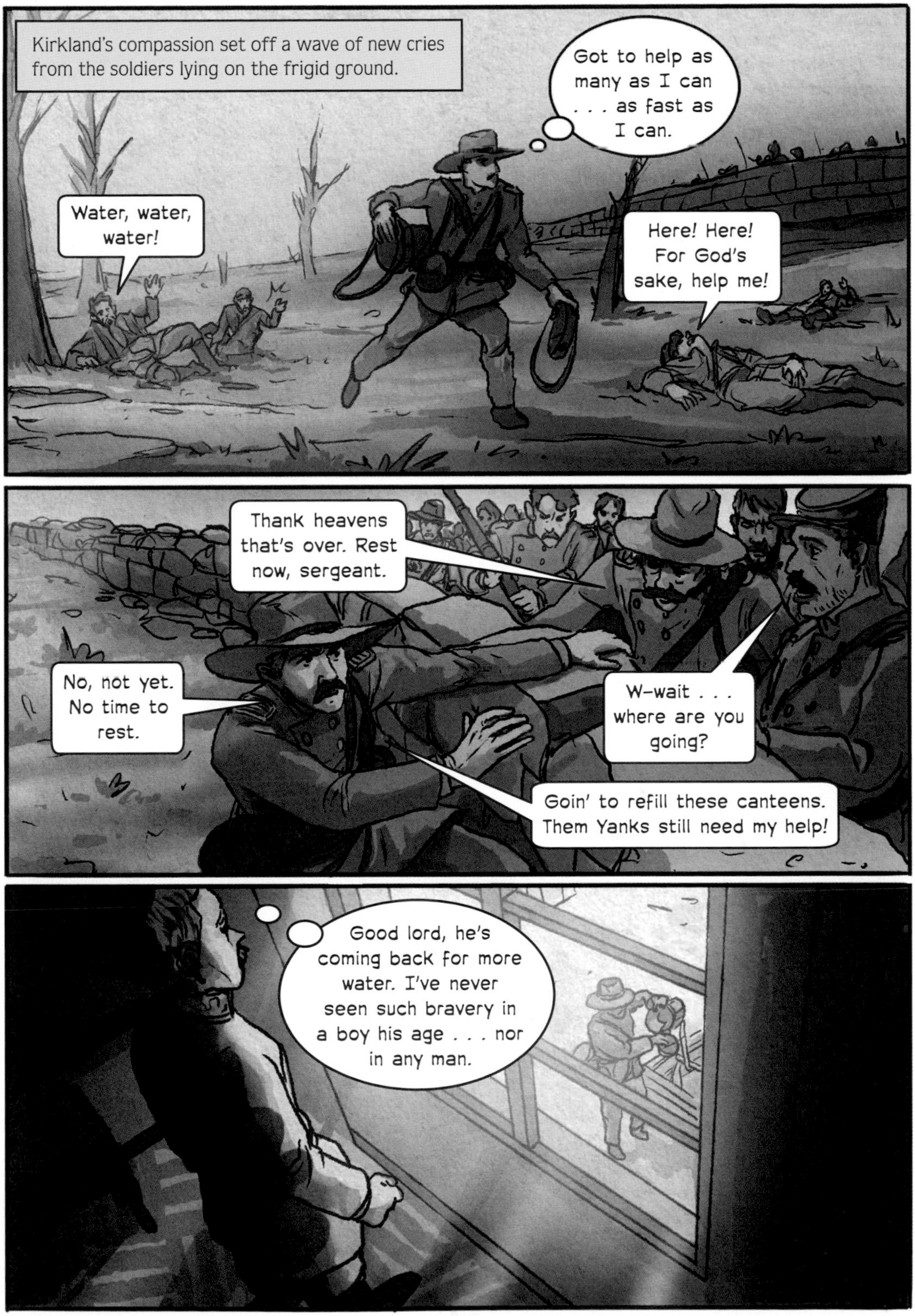
Kirkland's compassion set off a wave of new cries from the soldiers lying on the frigid ground.
Water, water, water!
Got to help as many as I can . . . as fast as I can.
Here! Here! For God's sake, help me!
Thank heavens that's over. Rest now, sergeant.
No, not yet. No time to rest.
W-wait . . . where are you going?
Goin' to refill these canteens. Them Yanks still need my help!
Good lord, he's coming back for more water. I've never seen such bravery in a boy his age . . . nor in any man.

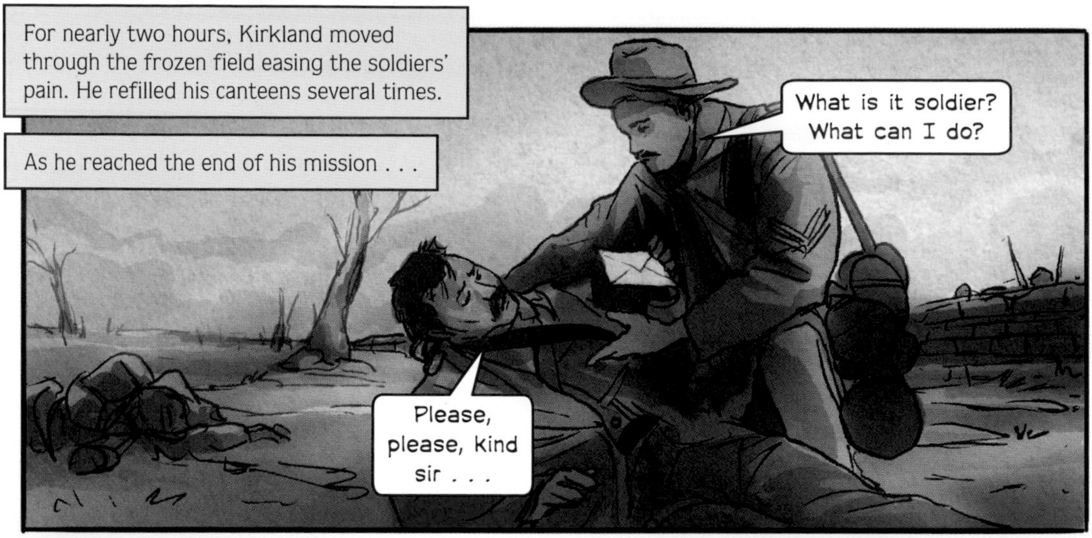
For nearly two hours, Kirkland moved through the frozen field easing the soldiers' pain. He refilled his canteens several times.
As he reached the end of his mission . . .
What is it soldier? What can I do?
Please, please, kind sir . . .

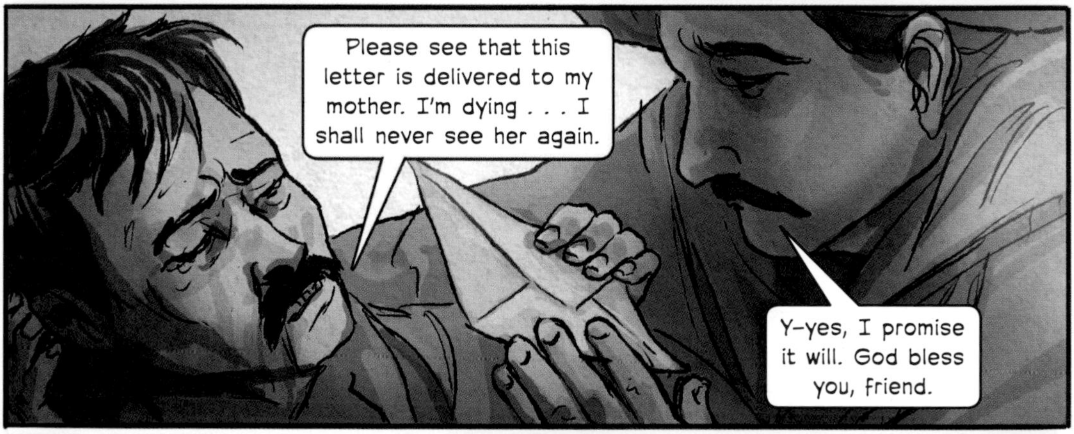
Please see that this letter is delivered to my mother. I'm dying . . . I shall never see her again.
Y-yes, I promise it will. God bless you, friend.

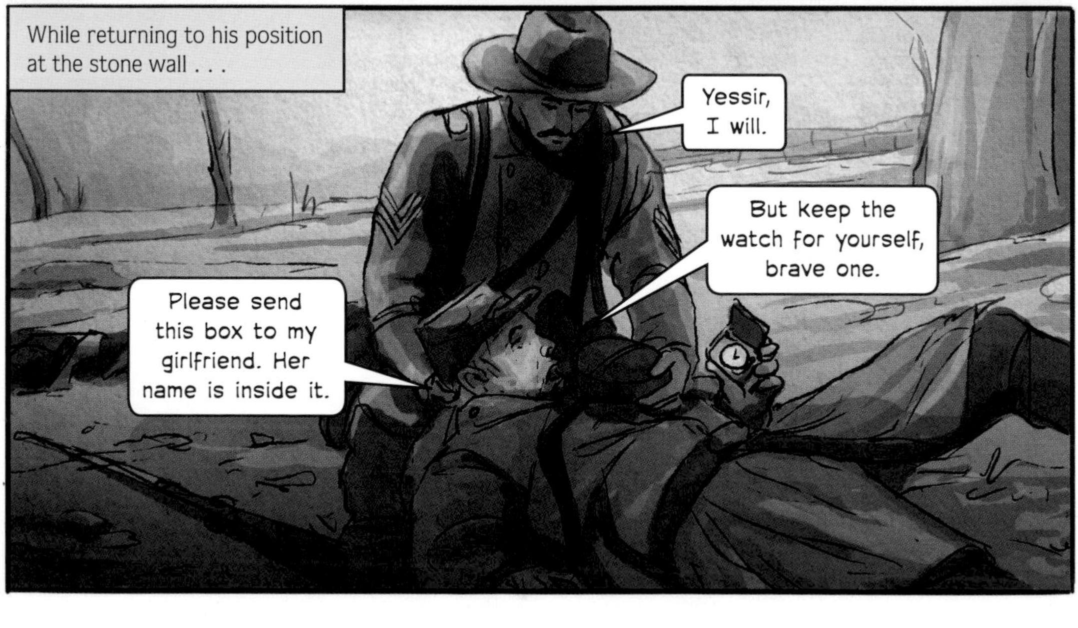
While returning to his position at the stone wall . . .
Please send this box to my girlfriend. Her name is inside it.
Yessir, I will.
But keep the watch for yourself, brave one.

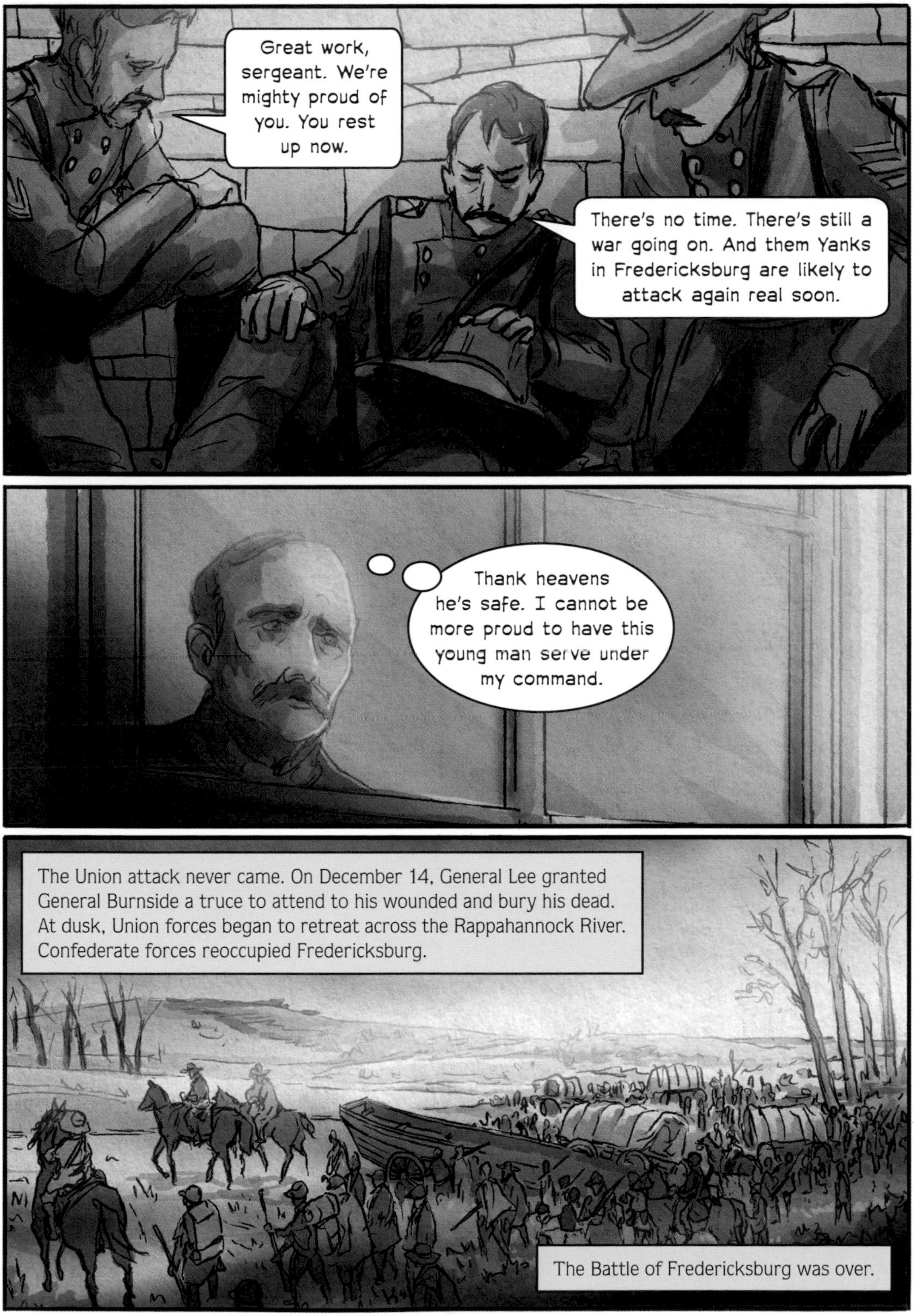
Great work, sergeant. We're mighty proud of you. You rest up now.
There's no time. There's still a war going on. And them Yanks in Fredericksburg are likely to attack again real soon.
Thank heavens he's safe. I cannot be more proud to have this young man serve under my command.
The Union attack never came. On December 14, General Lee granted General Burnside a truce to attend to his wounded and bury his dead. At dusk, Union forces began to retreat across the Rappahannock River. Confederate forces reoccupied Fredericksburg.
The Battle of Fredericksburg was over.

The Quality of Mercy

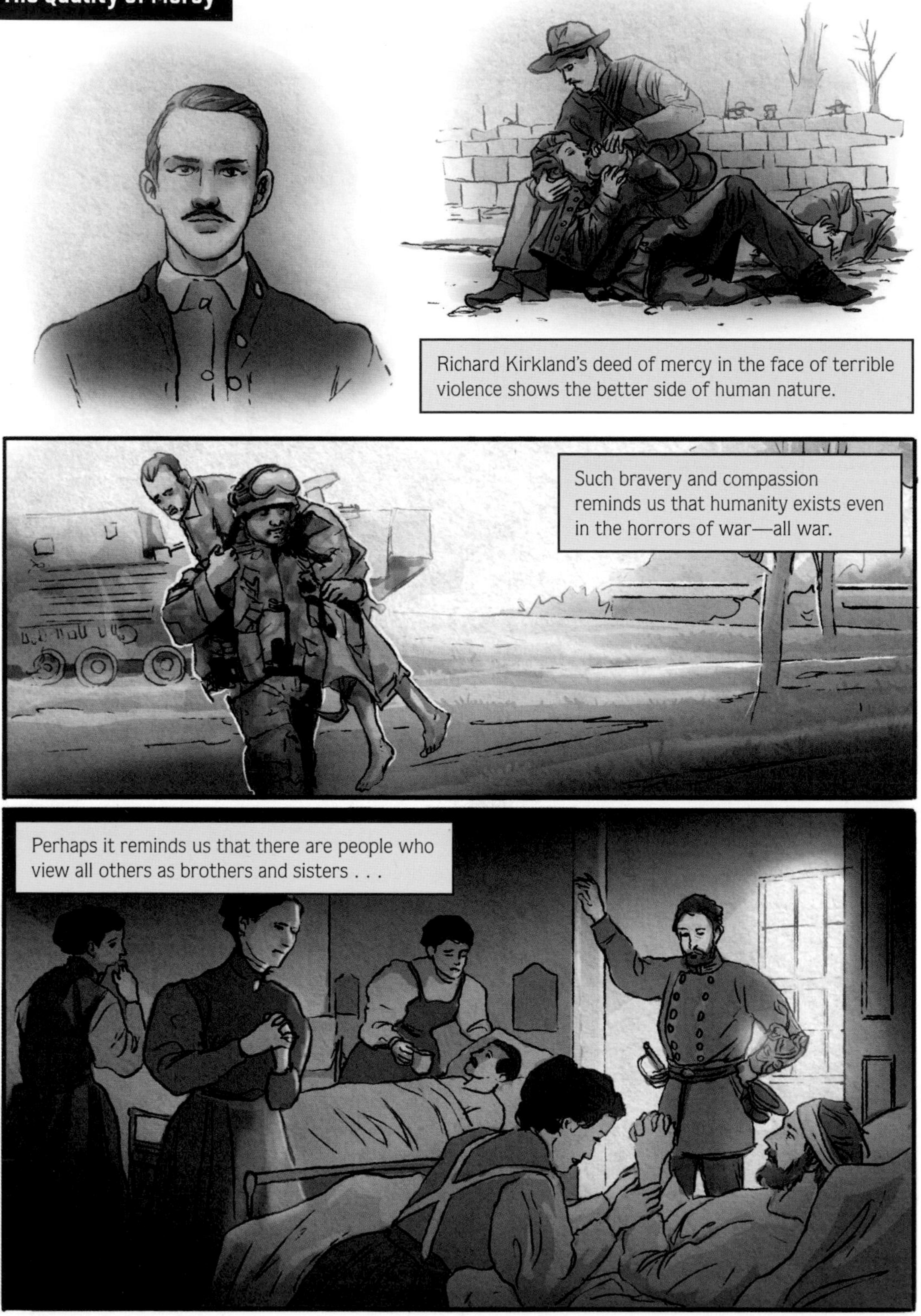

Richard Kirkland's deed of mercy in the face of terrible violence shows the better side of human nature.
Such bravery and compassion reminds us that humanity exists even in the horrors of war—all war.
Perhaps it reminds us that there are people who view all others as brothers and sisters . . .

. . . regardless of their differences, as large as they might seem.

A statue dedicated to Kirkland stands at the Fredericksburg and Spotsylvania National Military Park. It reads . . .

"At the risk of his life, this American soldier of sublime compassion brought water to his wounded foes at Fredericksburg. The fighting men on both sides of the line called him 'The Angel of Marye's Heights.' "

IN MEMORIAM
RICHARD ROWLAND KIRKLAND
CO. G. 2ND SOUTH CAROLINA VOLUNTEERS
C. S. A.
AT THE RISK OF HIS LIFE, THIS AMERICAN
SOLDIER OF SUBLIME COMPASSION BROUGHT
WATER TO HIS WOUNDED FOES AT
FREDERICKSBURG. THE FIGHTING MEN ON
BOTH SIDES OF THE LINE CALLED HIM
THE ANGEL OF MARYE'S HEIGHTS.

MORE ABOUT RICHARD ROWLAND KIRKLAND AND THE BATTLE OF FREDERICKSBURG

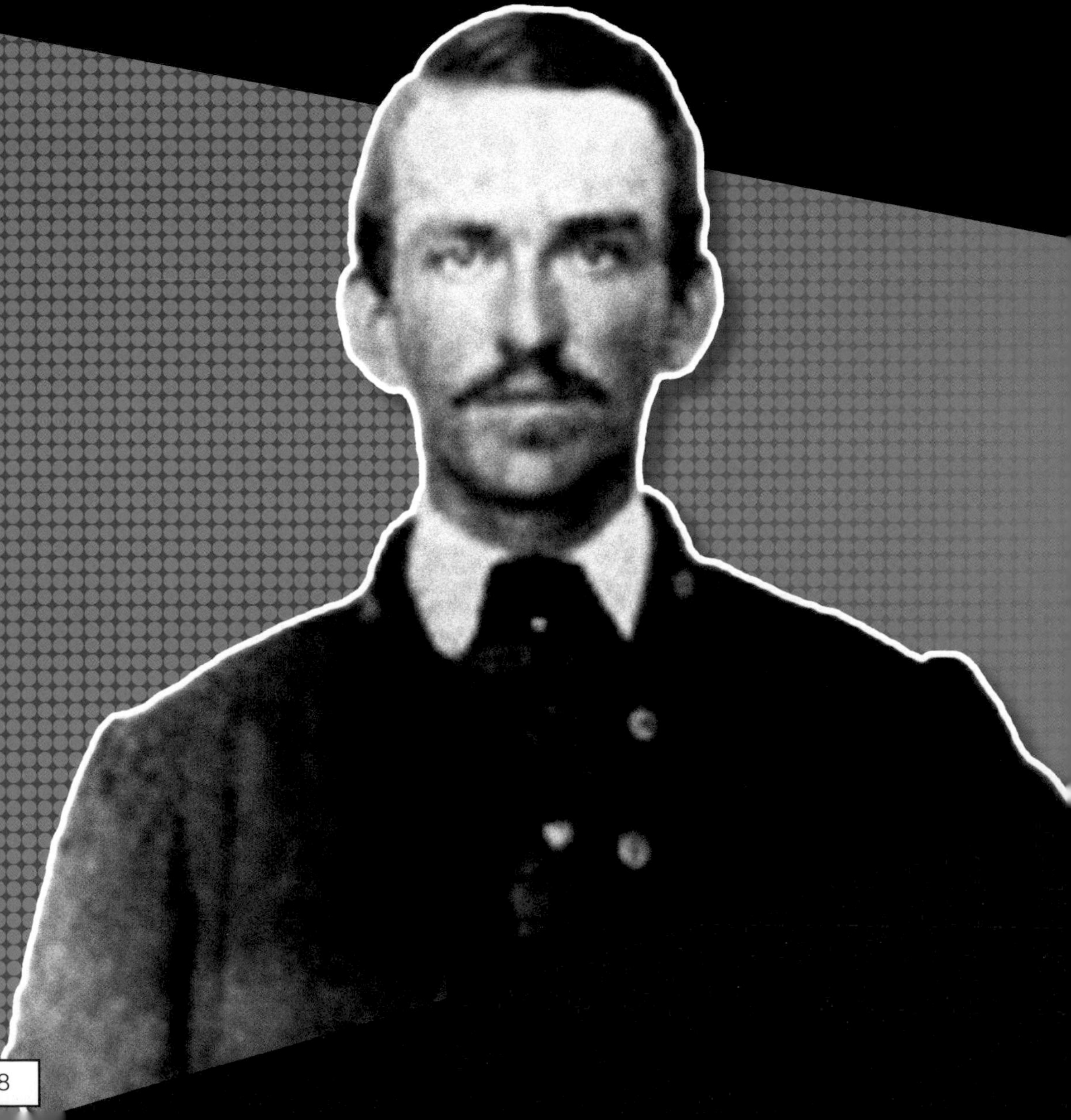

- Richard Rowland Kirkland's war did not end at Fredericksburg. He fought bravely at the Confederate victory at Chancellorsville in April–May 1863, and again at Gettysburg in July. General Kershaw promoted Kirkland to lieutenant for his outstanding service at Gettysburg.

- On September 20, 1863, Kirkland was shot and killed at the Battle of Chickamauga in Georgia. His dying words are said to be: "I am done for. You can do me no good. Save yourselves and please tell my pa I died right." He was barely 20 years old.

- The Battle of Fredericksburg produced joy and celebration for the Confederacy, but despair and sadness for the Union. The Union suffered more than 12,600 dead, wounded, or missing soldiers. Total Confederate losses were about 5,400 men. Witnessing the slaughter at Fredericksburg, Confederate general Robert E. Lee said, "It is well that war is so terrible. We should grow too fond of it."

- President Lincoln was sharply criticized for the Union defeat, even by his strongest supporters. Lincoln was deeply pained by the senseless, tragic loss of American soldiers on both sides. "If there is a worse place than hell, I am in it," he said.

- In late January 1863, Burnside requested to be relieved of command of the Union army. Lincoln granted his request, replacing him with Major General Joseph Hooker.

- Some historians claim the Kirkland story of mercy is untrue, or at least highly exaggerated. Most of the details of Kirkland's actions on December 14 come from a letter General Kershaw wrote to a newspaper in 1880—18 years after the battle.

- Over the years Kirkland has been celebrated in songs, poems, paintings, and stories. Today a monument honoring Kirkland's deeds stands at the Fredericksburg and Spotsylvania National Military Park. The monument was funded by private donations from the citizens of South Carolina and Virginia.

GLOSSARY

align (uh-LINE)—to put things in a straight line

artillery (ahr-TIL-ur-ee)—large, powerful guns that are mounted on wheels

devastate (DEV-uh-stayt)—to damage severely or destroy

diversion (di-VUR-zhuhn)—something meant to draw away someone's attention from something more important

flank (FLANGK)—the far left or right side of a group of soldiers

impenetrable (im-PEHN-uh-truh-bul)—impossible to pass through, break through, or enter

oblige (uh-BLIJE)—to do something because it is a law or a responsibility

overwhelm (oh-vur-WELM)—to defeat someone completely

rebellion (ri-BEL-yuhn)—armed fight against a government

relieve (ri-LEEV)—to take over someone's post, station, or duty

sublime (suh-BLIME)—excellence or greatness that inspires admiration or respect

truce (TROOS)—an agreement between enemies to stop fighting for a short time

READ MORE

Parker, Parker. *The Civil War Visual Encyclopedia*. New York: DK Publishing, 2021.

Roberts, Russell. *Turning Points of the Civil War*. Lake Elmo, MN: Focus Readers, 2020.

Smith, Elliott. *Hidden Heroes in the Civil War*. Minneapolis: Lerner Publications, 2023.

INTERNET SITES

The Angel of Marye's Heights: The SC State House
www.knowitall.org/photo/angel-maryes-heights-sc-state-house

Battle of Fredericksburg
www.ducksters.com/history/civil_war/battle_of_fredericksburg.php

Kirkland Memorial
www.nps.gov/places/kirkland-memorial.htm

ABOUT THE AUTHOR

Nel Yomtov is an award-winning author of children's nonfiction books and graphic novels. He specializes in writing about history, current events, biography, architecture, and military history. He has written numerous graphic novels for Capstone, including the recent *School Strike for Climate*, *Journeying to New Worlds: A Max Axiom Super Scientist Adventure*, and *Cher Ami: Heroic Carrier Pigeon of World War I*. In 2020 he self-published *Baseball 100*, an illustrated book featuring the 100 greatest players in baseball history. Nel lives in the New York City area.

ABOUT THE ILLUSTRATOR

Dante Ginevra's work can be found in numerous publications in his home country of Argentina. These include comics and comic strips in *Fierro*, *Télam*, and a variety of other magazines. In addition, he has illustrative work in graphic novels that span the globe. They include *Cardal*, published in Uruguay, and *Entreactos* and *El Muertero Zabaletta*, both published in Spain. Throughout his career he has also participated in numerous exhibitions in Argentina, Italy, Russia, Brazil, France, and Germany.